Invitation to FORTH

Invitation to FORTH

by Harry Katzan, Jr.
Consultant
Katzan International
Computer Consulting, Inc.

PBI
a petrocelli
book
new york / princeton

To Margaret, Kathy, and Karen

PREFACE

One of the latest entries to surface in the
ever changing universe of programming languages is
FORTH - a crisp straightforward language that
conveniently lends itself to the programming of
microcomputers. The FORTH programming language,
however, is not limited to microcomputer
applications and would be equally useful for
"larger" computers. In fact, the size or type of
computer is not at all significant to a prospective
user of FORTH. It is the availability of language
processing facilities that counts and currently,
most FORTH activity is centered in the
microcomputer area.

FORTH is more than another name in the already
long list of programming languages. FORTH is a
language for doing functional programming with a
specific orientation towards productivity,
reliability, and efficiency. Some of the concepts
associated with FORTH are structured programming,
top-down development, and virtual memory. However,
FORTH is not simply a focal point for popular
concepts. It represents a modern way of approaching
programming.

The structure of a FORTH program and the FORTH
language itself is based on reverse Polish notation
- or postfix notation, as some computer scientists
call it. This basic philosophy combined with an
effective definitional structure permits a high
degree of language flexibility and the ability to
customize the language to the requirements of a
particular application environment.

This book provides an introduction to the FORTH
language and is primarily intended for persons who
will program in the language, for persons who will
design systems and applications around the

language, and for persons that want to stay abreast of recent advances in computer technology. The subject matter includes a small amount of background material but otherwise plunges right into the FORTH language since it is the primary subject of the book.

The book is composed of ten chapters, outlined as follows:

Chapter 0: THE FORTH CONCEPT gives the basic idea of the language.

Chapter 1: COMPUTER FUNDAMENTALS gives a review of basic microcomputer concepts.

Chapter 2: SOFTWARE TECHNOLOGY covers the fundamentals of programming, software systems, and the development of computer applications.

Chapter 3: REVERSE POLISH NOTATION gives an overview of reverse Polish notation, the concept of a stack, and interpretive execution.

Chapter 4: ELEMENTARY CALCULATIONS AND STACK MANIPULATION covers the topics of arithmetic operators, number bases, stack operations, mathematical functions, and complement arithmetic.

Chapter 5: CONSTANTS, VARIABLES, AND STORAGE OPERATIONS covers how constants and variables are defined and used in FORTH, along with associated fetch and store operations.

Chapter 6: DEFINITIONS AND TERMINAL OPERATIONS covers the definitional facility in FORTH and the output operations provided to display information from within the computer.

Chapter 7: CONTROL STRUCTURES covers structured programming control structures and their representation in FORTH.

Chapter 8: DOUBLE PRECISION covers FORTH capability for handling double precision values and includes relevant operations delineated throughout the language.

Chapter 9: INFORMATION MANAGEMENT covers FORTH language features for storage organization and allocation, disk input and output, program management, character manipulation and keyboard operations, and output formatting and conversion.

The underlying objective of this book is to promote understanding of the FORTH concept. With this objective clearly in mind, the subject matter is presented through easy-to-read textual material liberally interspersed with examples. No particular background in either computers or programming is needed to completely understand the book and to learn the FORTH language. A general overview of computers, however, would be especially useful for recognizing the power and flexibility of the FORTH language. Moreover, the various topics are developed so that the reader can learn the FORTH language without necessarily having FORTH computer facilities at his or her disposal. Vocabulary lists are included for review, and exercises and answers are provided for each of the chapters.

This book should serve as a complete introduction to the FORTH language for computer professionals, engineers, business analysts, and the creative and energetic group of microcomputer enthusiasts. For rather obvious reasons, the systems-related aspects of FORTH were not covered and this includes the FORTH language processor, the editor, the run-time environment, and the extensibility features of the language. For information on these subjects, the interested reader should consult the FORTH Interest Group, P.O. Box 1105, San Carlos, California 94070.

The full potential of FORTH has really not been publicized and the language is continually evolving. Therefore, this book is being offered only as an invitation to a productive future. The user's guide for a particular implementation of FORTH should serve as the definitive reference for the construction of actual programs.

As much as possible, this book was produced using microcomputer text-processing facilities, and is a genuine effort to provide timely information on an important topic for interested people. The author and the publisher have thoroughly enjoyed producing the book and sincerely hope the reader will enjoy learning the FORTH language as much as we have enjoyed bringing it to you. Happy programming!

It is a pleasure to acknowledge the cooperation and assistance of several people: to Mr. O.R. Petrocelli, the publisher, for useful suggestions and the foresight and courage to publish a book on the groundbreaking subject of the FORTH language; to Bruce Tucker for timely information when it was needed; and to my wife, Margaret, for handling the word-processing aspects of the job, for spending long tedious hours on the production of camera ready copy, and for being a good partner during the entire project.

Harry Katzan, Jr.
Stillhouse Road
Freehold, N.J. 07728
January, 1981

CONTENTS

Chapter 0. THE FORTH CONCEPT

FORTH is a crisp easy-to-learn language that makes the otherwise complex process of computer programming very straightforward and very simple. FORTH is efficient, which means that programs written in the FORTH language execute quickly on the computer. FORTH is also user friendly, which means that once you learn the fundamental language concepts, it helps you write a program rather than getting in your way. Using FORTH can be as simple as using a hand calculator, but programs written in the language can represent complex algorithmic processes normally requiring a programming language much more difficult to learn than FORTH.

CALCULATORS AND FORTH

The everyday hand calculator is a convenient means of simplifying calculations and achieves its greatest value from compactness, mobility, simplicity of use, and relevance to a particular class of problems. An automatic computer, on the other hand, has a different problem domain, so that its characteristics are quite dissimilar from that of a calculator. A computer has a high degree of flexibility and generality of use, but at the same time is operationally complex. In fact, many programming languages have been developed to span the man-machine interface and to take advantage of the versatility and speed of automatic computers. The FORTH programming language combines the two concepts in such a manner that the user has available the power and flexibility of an automatic computer with the convenience of a hand calculator.

MATHEMATICAL NOTATION

Mathmatical notation for arithmetic operations in calculators usually takes either of two familiar forms:

    o Algebraic entry notation
    o Reverse Polish notation

Algebraic entry notation is characterized by the fact that arithmetic calculations are performed when they are entered, as demonstrated in the following key sequence:

$$7 + 12 =$$

that would display a result of 19. Whereas, a key sequence of

$$2 + 3 X 4 =$$

would yield a result of 20. The result may be surprising; however, it should be remembered that the addition is executed first because it is entered first. The calculations take place in an "accumulator" which holds the result displayed. In some calculators with algebraic entry notation, parentheses are allowed, as in the evaluation of (6-3)X(10-5) that would be keyed in algebraic notation as

$$(6 - 3) X (10 - 5) =$$

This key sequence would yield a result of 15. Algebraic entry notation is characterized by the fact that the arithmetic operator symbol is placed between the numbers, as in 2+2.

    Another approach to the representation of arithmetic expressions is to use Reverse Polish Notation (RPN), wherein the arithmetic operator follows both members of a two-number operation, as in

$$3 ENTER 2 +$$

which is a representation of 3+2. One of the advantages of RPN is that fewer keystrokes are required for complex operations. The evaluation of (6-3)X(10-5) would be keyed in RPN as:

6 ENTER 3 - 10 ENTER 5 - X

The use of Reverse Polish Notation is similar to
the way arithmetic is performed on some calculators
and with many adding machines. The FORTH system
employs Reverse Polish Notation, which is covered
in chapter three. If you already know it, then you
can skip that chapter.

OPERATIONAL ENVIRONMENT

FORTH is an interactive language which means
that as soon as FORTH comes up on your screen, you
can begin to interact with the system. There are
two modes of operation in FORTH:

    o The execution mode
    o The definition mode

In the execution mode, you get action whenever you
enter a series of calculations or a procedure
reference. In the definition mode, a series of
commands are saved for subsequent reference. Thus,
FORTH can be used with equal ease for simple
calculations and for complex programs.

THE STACK

A stack is a means of organizing data so that
the last item entered is the first item retrieved.
Several means of conceptualizing a stack are
possible:

    o As a stack of dishes in a cafeteria
    o As a pile of documents

The notion of a stack is not uncommon in the
computer field. Some computers and a fair amount
of software are designed around the stack concept.
In many cases, a computer user is not even aware of

the fact that a stack is being employed. In other words, the stack is transparent to the user.
    FORTH uses a stack to hold items of data and it is not transparnt to the user. Data items are entered into the stack directly. Then when an operation or a procedure reference comes along, it is always executed on values from the stack. In FORTH, the programmer controls the stack and explicitly places values in it.

FORTH OPERATIONS

    In FORTH, an expression such as:

4+3

is written in reverse Polish notation so that it becomes:

4 3 +

FORTH executes the reverse Polish expression from left to right. When a data value is encountered, it is placed in the stack by "pushing down" values that are below it. This is why a stack is commonly referred to as a "pushdown stack." The use of the word "pushdown" is clearly redundant since a stack, by its very nature, is a pushdown device.
    The following graphics depict the operation of a stack with the reverse Polish expression given above:

TOP	-	4	3	7
STACK	-	-	4	-
	-	-	-	-
EXPRESSION	(Empty)	4	3	+

One fact about the use of a stack is obvious from
this example.   When an operation is performed, it
uses   up the needed values from the top of the stack
and "pushes" the result back on the stack.

EXECUTION MODE

When an expresssion is entered into the FORTH
system, the characters are typed as in the example.
When the RETURN key is pressed, FORTH performs the
specified   computer   operations   and generates
whatever output is specified. FORTH then looks for
the next user input.   Here is an example as you
would actually see it on the computer's screen:

    <u>4 3 +</u> OK

The underlined material represents what the user
would type in and the remainder of the line is
generated by the FORTH system. In this case, the
calculation did not yield any output so FORTH
responded with an OK indicating that the last
command was successfully completed and FORTH is now
ready for additional commands.   In case you
wondered what happened to the result in the last
example, FORTH left it on the top of the stack. In
order to have it displayed, a {.} , pronounced
"dot", would have to be used as follows:

    <u>4 3 + .</u> 7 OK

(Note: Braces {} are used to isolate FORTH words in
the text when their meaning could otherwise be
confusing.)   The dot command simply displays the
top value on the stack. After the display, the
value is removed from the stack, as shown by the
following example:

7 3 9 4 . . . . 4 9 3 7 OK

This example reflects the last-in-first-out
property of a stack. The number 4 was entered last
and displayed first. After it was displayed and
removed from the stack, then 9 was displayed, and
so forth. Values are left in the stack between
FORTH statements, as demonstrated in the following
script:

5 9 2 OK

- . . . 7 5 0   EMPTY STACK

In the latter case, the final 0 was displayed
because the stack was empty when FORTH encountered
the final dot command. This fact is explicitly
indicated with the message EMPTY STACK.

DEFINITION MODE

     A procedure in the FORTH language is actually a
command that is executed when it is encountered in
an input line. When a procedure is defined, it is
given a name. That name is used to execute the
procedure.
     A procedure definition begins with a colon {:}
and ends with a semicolon {;}. In between is the
procedure name followed by the commands and values
that comprise the procedure. Because procedures
always start with a {:}, they are known in FORTH as
"colon definitions."
     A colon definition of a simple procedure that
multiplies the value on top of the stack by 2 is
given as follows:

: DOUBLE 2 * ; OK

DOUBLE, when executed, places the value 2 in the
stack pushing down the value currently on top. The
operator {*}, which represents multiplication,
forms the product of the top two stack entries,

removing them, and placing the product in the
stack. In the following example:

   125 DOUBLE . 250 OK
   _____

the following sequence of steps is executed: (1)
The value 125 is placed on the stack. (2) The
procedure DOUBLE is invoked, which pushes the value
2 into the stack, multiplies the two top stack
items - also removing them - and placing the
product of 250 on the stack. (3) The top item on
the stack - i.e., 250 - is displayed and removed
from the stack.

     Colon definitions are a powerful tool for the
FORTH programmer.   One colon definition can
reference another colon definition and this nesting
process   can effectively be used to implement
top-down development and modular programming. Most
procedures   or   commands   - defined by colon
definitions or existing as a primitive in the FORTH
language - work exactly the same as commands
entered in the execution mode or as components in
other colon definitions.

              ADDITIONAL FORTH CAPABILITY

     The preceding information gives only the FORTH
concept   and   the reader is cautioned against
thinking that this is all there is to the language.
The subject matter presented in this chapter gives
only a taste of the language and does not even
serve as an overview.   Subsequent chapters cover
the following key topics:

     o Computer Fundamentals
     o Software Technology
     o Reverse Polish Notation
     o Elementary Calculations and Stack
         Manipulation
     o Constants, Variables, and Memory Operations
     o Definitions and Terminal Operations

    o Control Structures
    o Double Precision
    o Information Management

For each topic, the structure of the various FORTH
commands and statements and the manner in which the
FORTH system responds to this input are covered in
detail.

VOCABULARY

    A general familiarity with the following terms
will help in learning the FORTH language:

Algebraic entry notation
Colon definition
Definition mode
Execution mode
OK
Reverse Polish notation
Stack

EXERCISES

1. Evaluate the following expressions
    in reverse Polish notation:

        6 12 +
        3 5 * 2 +
        3 3 * 4 4 * +

2. Execute the following FORTH state-
    ments:

        3 7 * .
        3 6 2 9 + + + .
        3 6 2 + 9 . . .

3. Given the following colon defini-
    tions:

```
: DOUBLE 2 * ;

: 4TIMES DOUBLE DOUBLE ;
```

Execute the following FORTH statements:

```
4 5 DOUBLE + .

3 4TIMES 1 + .
```

Chapter 1. COMPUTER FUNDAMENTALS

Computer Philosophy

Computer Memory

Hardware, Software, and Firmware

Microcomputer Systems Organization

Microprocessor Organization and Operation

Stack Operation

Disk Storage Technology

Vocabulary

Exercises

Computers are frequently regarded as "black boxes" by people who use them. With the black box concept, the major concern is over the input, outputs, and functions of a system. Knowledge of the components within the black box is normally left to specialists. The approach is not unusual in today's world of advanced technology. Clearly, computers are not being singled out here, and the concept applies equally well to automobiles, television receivers, radars, powerful hand calculators, many household appliances, and so forth. One of the factors contributing to the microcomputer revolution, however, is the simple fact that a person does not have to be an electronics expert in order to utilize a computer effectively. The FORTH language continues in the above direction by making it relatively easy to program a computer without possessing full detailed knowledge of the computer being used. On the other hand, some computer background is needed to fully utilize the features in FORTH. This chapter provides a survey of computer fundamentals. Many engineers and computer people already know everything presented in this chapter, and they can skip it. Others may wish to browse through the chapter filling in their background as needed. The subject matter of this chapter has been specially selected for this book on the FORTH language. For example, microcomputer organization, the microprocessor, stack operation, and disk storage technology are included because they are the topics with which the FORTH programmer will deal most frequently. Other topics, such as video displays and printer technology, are not covered at all because detailed knowledge of those subjects does not specifically help in writing FORTH programs.

COMPUTER PHILOSOPHY

At this time, two philosophies exist for the design and construction of digital computers:

o The Harvard architecture
o The Princeton architecture

In both forms of computer architecture, the machine
features contain the same basic elements:

The INPUT MECHANISM used to enter programs and
data into the computer

The MEMORY CONCEPT used to store instructions
and data while the computer is in operation

The ARITHMETIC/LOGIC UNIT for performing
calculations

The CONTROL UNIT for allowing the computer to
operate automatically by interpreting
instructions, going from one instruction to its
successor, and by permitting the computer to
select alternatives based on computed results

The OUTPUT MECHANISM used to transfer data from
the computer to the external world

The difference between the two philosophies exists
in the "memory concept." In a Harvard machine, the
program memory and the data memory are separate.
In fact, the Harvard Mark I calculator was
controlled by a program on punched paper tape and
contained an internal electromechanical data
storage capacity of only sixty 23-digit numbers.
Subsequent machines in the Harvard class were
controlled by either electromechanical switches or
by electrical connectors called plug boards.
      In a Princeton machine - also known as the von
Neumann machine - instructions and data are stored
in the same form in the same computer memory. The
potential benefit from this philosophy is obvious.
With the Princeton machine, a high degree of
flexibility is achieved because a computing machine
can then change the very instructions that control
it.
      Most existing computers are Princeton machines.

However, the widespread use of high-level
programming languages and the logical separation of
a program into a "program part" and a "data part"
have diminished the primary advantage of the
Princeton architecture. Modern microcomputers have
taken a big step toward combining the two
philosophies by utilizing more than one kind of
memory.

COMPUTER MEMORY

The primary function of the computer memory is
to hold instructions and data so that they can be
recalled when necessary during the execution of the
computer. We are talking here about internal
memory (also called main memory or main storage)
and not about external storage mechanisms, such as
tape cassettes or revolving disk mediums. Computer
memory is divided into two classes: ROM and RAM.
ROM stands for Read-Only Memory and it is used to
hold programs and a small amount of data that do
not change during the course of computer operation.
When you turn on a microcomputer, for example, it
responds immediately. This feat happens because
the computer is being controlled by a program in
ROM. (In large computers, ROM is known as control
storage, but is used in a different manner than
with microcomputers.) ROM memory cannot be
modified by a user program and when the power to
the computer is turned off, the contents of ROM
remain intact. Information is placed on a ROM chip
when the chip is fabricated. PROM, which stands
for programmable read-only memory, is a variation
to ROM which can be loaded by the user either
through special programming or by unique electrical
or optical equipment. When information is placed
on a PROM chip, it is said to be "burned in," and
the portion of the PROM chip that has been altered
cannot be changed. It is possible to program one
part of a PROM chip at one time and other parts at
later times. Regardless of whether ROM or PROM is
being used, it cannot be changed after it is

written.   A third type of read-only memory is
EPROM,   which   stands   for   Erasable Programmable
Read-Only Memory.   An EPROM can be programmed,
erased, and then reprogrammed.   EPROMs, however,
are relatively inexpensive.   In this book, ROM,
PROM,   and EPROM are referred to collectively as
ROM.   Regardless of whether ROM, PROM, or EPROM is
being used, the appearance to the user is exactly
the same: the computer responds immediately to the
user through its collection of "built-in" programs.

RAM,   which   stands for random-access memory, is
used to hold the user's program and data. The name
"random   access   memory" refers to the fact that the
speed of the memory is independent of the location
being referenced, and this property holds for ROM,
as well.   When the power to the computer is turned
off, the contents of RAM are lost.

RAM   comes in two varieties: static and dynamic.
With static RAM, information is stored by setting
"flip flop" electronic devices.   Information in
static RAM is retained until it is either changed
by a program or the power to the computer is turned
off.   With dynamic RAM, information is stored
through electrical charges that dissipate and must
be refreshed - hence the name "dynamic" RAM. In
most cases, dynamic RAM is preferable because fewer
electronic components are needed resulting in a
smaller and less expensive package. Dynamic RAMs
are also faster and use less power on the average.
The refreshing operation is normally handled by the
microprocessor   or by special circuitry and is
transparent to the user.

The amount of computer memory referenced during
one   memory   access   is   called   BANDWIDTH.
(Frequently, bandwidth is used synonomously with
the term "word size.") In the design of ROM and
RAM, the bandwidth is usually set at an optimum
trade-off level for instructions and data. One of
the options available to computer designers is to
have separate memories for instructions and data,
allowing an optional bandwidth for each case. This
is another instance of Harvard architecture. For
example, consider an application domain - such as

automobile electronics - where the microcomputer is
to operate on 4 bit quantities. The use of memory
can be optimized by having a word size (i.e.,
bandwidth) for instructions of 8 bits and a word
size for data of 4 bits. This subject has been
discussed most recently (see Crazon [1]) for the
design of single chip microcomputers. Another fact
reported by Crazon that may be surprising to many
microcomputer users is that a microcomputer needs
from 16 to 32 times more memory for instructions
than for data. This is obviously the case because
of the applications for which microcomputers are
used.   The need for large tables and arrays is not
common and in the few cases where large memory
requirement do exist - say in the area of high
resolution graphics - the programs are
correspondingly large.   Also, the cost of RAM to
ROM ranges from 4:1 to 8:1. The result is obvious:
it pays to conserve RAM.
    The key point to be recognized here is that the
FORTH language is "right on the button" for
microcomputer applications.   FORTH contains
extensive and efficient facilities for data
manipulation, but has a relatively limited
capability for handling tables and arrays and
high-volume input/output operations.

HARDWARE, SOFTWARE, AND FIRMWARE

    Three terms are employed to identify facilities
inherent in a computer system: hardware, software,
and firmware.   Hardware designates the physical
components of the system - such as microprocessors,
memories, disk drives, and tape units. Software
designates the various sets of instructions used to
control the operation of the computer. Software is
usually recorded in the computer system as
electrical impulses in one form or another, but it
is not a physical device - hence the name software.
Firmware designates instructions, normally stored
in ROM or executed out of ROM, that determine how
the hardware operates or greatly facilitates using

the computer. The name firmware apparently stems from the notion of software that is "firmly" stored in ROM.

The origin of the term firmware comes from large-scale computers wherein the control unit of a computer is programmed to use the other components in a prescribed fashion. This process, known as microprogramming, is employed to synthesize machine instructions from basic hardware components such as switches, adders, registers, and control circuits. The use of firmware and microprogramming is an alternative in computer design to "hard wiring" the computer. The key point is that instructions stored in ROM were regarded as firmware and the concept has been extended through normal usage to apply to microcomputer instructions stored in and executed out of ROM.

MICROCOMPUTER SYSTEMS ORGANIZATION

A microcomputer system is a set of compatible components that operate under the control of a microprocessor. The microprocessor is the main component in the system and also performs the processing. The total organization of the system is suggested by Figure 1.1, which gives a block diagram of a typical microcomputer system containing the following components:

> Microprocessor
> Read-only memory
> Random-access memory
> Keyboard interface
> Video display interface
> Disk system controller
> Printer interface
> Cassette interface

The microprocessor is commonly known as "the computer on a chip," although in reality, it is only the processing element that resides on that chip. A single chip can contain thousands of

transistors and other discrete devices - hence the
name integrated circuit. Modern integrated
circuits are densely packed and known as Large
Scale Integrated circuits(LSIs). Each of the other
components in the system is synthesized from one or
more integrated circuit chips.

Another important element in a microcomputer is
the bus used to transport information between
components of the computer and usually exist in
microcomputers as either 8-bit and most recently
16-bit data lines. The address bus sends "address"
information from the microprocessor to the various
components while the data bus is used to transfer
data between the components and the microprocessor.

In Figure 1.1, the memories and the
input/output units share the same bus, so that the
microprocessor can treat an input/output device as
another memory device. In other microcomputer
systems, there is a separate bus for the memory and
for the input/output units.

MICROPROCESSOR ORGANIZATION AND OPERATION

A microprocessor operates by executing
instructions held in RAM or ROM. Normally, RAM and
ROM have the same address space so each responds in
exactly the same manner to the microprocessor. In
a general fashion, the operation of a
microprocessor proceeds as follows:

1. An instruction is fetched from either RAM or
ROM

2. The instruction is decoded to determine the
operation and the operands

3. The operands are retrieved from either RAM
or ROM

4. The specified operation is executed

In order to perform the above tasks, the

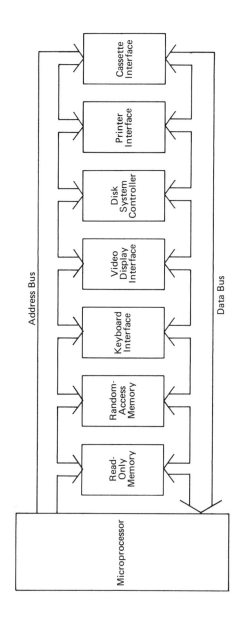

Figure 1.1
Block diagram of a typical microcomputer system.

microprocessor requires internal read/write memory
for its operation. This internal read/write memory
is divided into "registers" - each with a specific
purpose. They are described later. During the
performance of these tasks, the operation of the
microprocessor is organized into two cycles:

     o The instruction cycle (I-cycle)
     o The execution cycle (E-cycle)

Steps 1 and 2 take place during the instruction
cycle; steps 3 and 4 take place during the
execution cycle. Clearly, one occurrence of each
cycle is needed to execute one machine instruction
so that a machine cycle is defined as an I-cycle
followed by an E-cycle.
     The implementation of machine cycle processing
within a microprocessor requires three major
elements: a control unit, an arithmetic/logic unit,
and a set of machine registers. A block diagram of
a typical microprocessor is given in Figure 1.2,
which shows the interrelationship of the various
elements.
     The microprocessor registers are usually
configured as static RAM within the microprocessor.
Some registers can be addressed by an executing
program; others are under the control of the
microprocessor and are normally not referenced
directly by a program.
     Registers not normally addressed directly by
the user are the instruction register, the program
counter, the stack pointer, the memory address
register, the memory data register, and the memory
refresh register. The INSTRUCTION REGISTER is used
by the control unit of the microprocessor to decode
and interpret an instruction. After an instruction
is fetched from RAM or ROM, it is routed via an
internal data bus to the instruction register,
where the fields in an instruction word are
isolated by the circuitry of the control unit. The
PROGRAM COUNTER (often referred to as the CURRENT
ADDRESS REGISTER) is used by the control unit to
keep track of the address in RAM or ROM of the

current instruction. When it is time to fetch an
instruction, the control unit goes to the program
counter to determine its location. During the
execution of an instruction by the microprocessor,
the program counter is incremented by the length
attribute of the instruction so that the succeeding
instruction is executed next. The STACK POINTER is
a register that holds the address of the current
position of the top of the stack. Normally, the
stack is not located in the read/write memory of
the microprocessor but in RAM memory external to
the microprocessor. Two registers are needed to
reference RAM and ROM. The Memory Address Register
(MAR) contains the address of the word to be
written to or read from memory. The Memory Data
Register (MDR) holds the data word before it is
written to memory or after it is read from memory.
As reflected in the block diagram of a typical
microprocessor (Figure 1.2), the memory address
register deals with "data address control" and the
memory data register deals with "data bus control."
Figure 1.3 gives the flow of instructions and data
within the microprocessor. Some microprocessors
also include a MEMORY REFRESH REGISTER for keeping
count of the refresh operation for dynamic RAM.
When a memory refresh register is present in a
microprocessor, it can be loaded under program
control for hardware testing purposes but is
normally not used by the programmer.

Registers addressed directly by the user are
the accumulator, index registers, and
general-purpose registers. The ACCUMULATOR holds
results of arithmetic and logical operations by the
arithmetic/logic unit and serves as one of the
inputs to the arithmetic/logic unit for most
microprocessor operations. The INDEX REGISTERS are
used for addressing - usually with array data.
GENERAL PURPOSE REGISTERS hold addresses and data
during processing and frequently serve as a second
input to the arithmetic/logic unit. Figure 1.4
gives a block diagram of data flow during the
operation of the arithmetic/logic unit.

Most microprocessors also contain a variety of

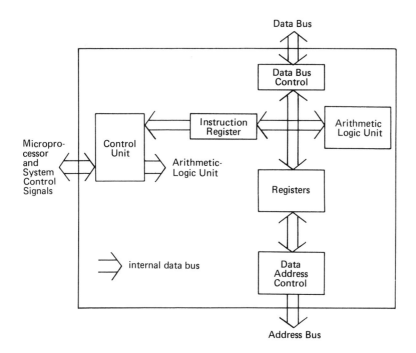

Figure 1.2
General Block diagram of a typical microprocessor

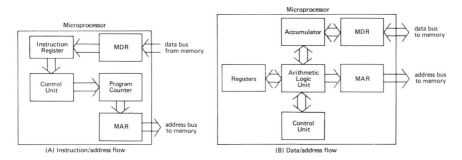

Figure 1.3
Flow of instructions and data within a microprocessor

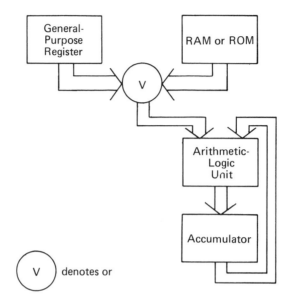

Figure 1.4
Data flow during arithmetic/logic unit processing

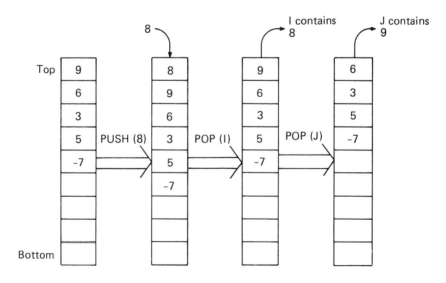

Figure 1.5
Conceptual view of stack operation.

status registers and "flag" registers that are set during normal computer operation by the hardware and can be tested and cleared by a user's program.

STACK OPERATION

A stack is a set of registers whose contents are managed on a last-in-first-out (LIFO) basis. As mentioned previously, the stack can be implemented in the microprocessor itself or in RAM memory. Two aspects of a stack are important:

     o The size (length) of the stack
     o The stack pointer

The two entities go together. The number of bits in the stack pointer determines the maximum capacity of the stack. For example, if the width of the stack pointer is 3 bits, then the stack can hold eight entries, numbered 0 through 7. Two computer operations are normally designed to manipulate the stack: push and pop. The PUSH operation places an entry in the stack, and as an entry is made, the previous entries are pushed down. The POP operation removes an entry from the stack, and as the removal is performed, the previous entries are pushed up. Figure 1.5 gives a conceptual view of stack operation.

A stack is commonly used with arithmetic and logical operations and for saving the return addresses for calls to subprograms. Because a stack is finite in size, the stack can overflow if too many entries are pushed into it. When this occurs, the "earliest" entry is lost, as described in Figure 1.6.

When a stack is implemented in RAM, the stack pointer moves up and down as PUSH and POP operations are executed. This method of implementing a stack is demonstrated in Figure 1.7 and Figure 1.8 gives Pascal procedures for the PUSH and POP operations. In the procedures, STACK is an array of integers whose subscripts range from 0 to

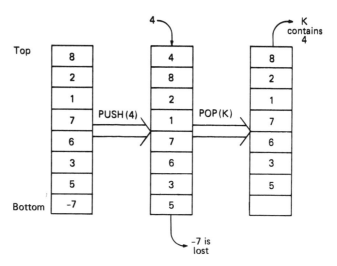

Figure 1.6
Stack overflow

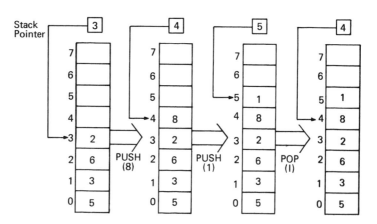

Figure 1.7
Implementation of a stack.

```
PROCEDURE PUSH(VALUE: INTEGER);
  BEGIN
    PT:= PT+1;
    IF PT>7 THEN
      PT:=0;
    STACK[PT]:=VALUE
  END;


PROCEDURE POP(VAR ENTRY: INTEGER);
  BEGIN
    IF PT<0
      THEN
        BEGIN
          ENTRY:=0;
          WRITE('STACK IS EMPTY')
        END
      ELSE
        BEGIN
          ENTRY:=STACK[PT];
          PT:=PT-1;
          IF PT<0 THEN
            PT:=7
        END
  END;
```

Figure 1.8
Pascal procedures for stack operations.

7 and PT is a stack pointer. Both STACK and PT are
declared   as   global   variables.   The   following
procedure calls would yield the results indicated:

    CALL   RESULT

    PUSH(8)   Places 8 in the stack
    PUSH(-7)   Places -7 in the stack
    PUSH(5)   Places 5 in the stack
    POP(I)   Removes 5 from the stack and
                    places it in I

Stack   operation   and   reverse   Polish   notation are
covered in more detail in chapter 3.

                    DISK STORAGE TECHNOLOGY

     The   processing   capability   of   modern computer
systems   is directly related to the speed with which
data   can be transferred in and out of the computer.
The   transfer   rate   with   serial   devices,   such as
tape,   is   inherently   limited because it is usually
necessary   to pass over preceding information before
the   needed   information can be accessed. With disk
storage,   data   can   be   accessed   directly without
having   to space over preceding information while at
the   same   time   providing   the   capability   for
sequential access.
     A   magnetic   disk recording medium is a circular
disc   coated   with magnetic recording material. The
concept   is   similar to that of a phonograph record,
because   data   is   recorded on tracks and is read or
written   as   the   disk   rotates.   The   tracks on a
magnetic   disk   are   concentric,   whereas   on   a
phonograph   record, they are spiral. The speed of a
magnetic   disk   unit   stems from the manner in which
data   are   accessed. A read/write head moves to the
correct   track   and   only   then does a data transfer
operation   take   place. (This operation is known as
direct   access.)   Disk   storage   comes   in two
varieties: hard   disk   and soft disk. HARD DISK is
characterized   by the fact that the recording medium

is a set of metal disks, coated with magnetic
material, and mounted on a rotating spindle. A
single disk is approximately 14 inches in diameter.
The stack of disks is referred to as a DISK VOLUME,
and if the volume is removable, it is called a DISK
PACK. Data are recorded on both surfaces of a disk
(except perhaps the top and bottom surfaces of a
volume, which are used for protection) and a single
arm controls two read/write heads - one for the
upper surface and one for the lower surface. The
access arms for a comb-type assembly move in and
out together, and a single read/write head is used
to access an entire surface. If the access arms
and read/write heads are in a sealed assembly with
the magnetic disks, then the unit is known as a
WINCHESTER DISK. Hard disks are predominantly used
with medium to large-scale computers.

A SOFT DISK is flexible and is usually called a
FLOPPY DISK or a DISKETTE. A diskette is either an
eight-inch or a five-inch circular piece of flat
Mylar [TM] polyester sheathed in a polyvinyl
chloride protective jacket - resembling a 45 rpm
phonograph record. The eight-inch variety is
commonly used with small business computers. The
five-inch variety is frequently used with
development systems and with personal/home/hobby
computers. Each recording track on a diskette is
divided into equally-sized zones called SECTORS.
Thus, an area of a diskette is identified by a
track number and a sector number.

A diskette can be hard sectored or soft
sectored. A soft-sector formatted diskette has
magnetically recorded sector locations, whereas a
hard-sector formatted diskette has sector locations
indicated with holes actually punched through the
disk surface.

A typical five-inch diskette has the following
characteristics:

   Number of tracks: 35
   Number of sectors per track: 13
   Number of bytes per sector: 250
   Total capacity: approximately 116,000 bytes

Figure 1.9 gives a diagram of a typical diskette.

Disk storage is used in a unique way in FORTH. An entire disk is divided into blocks of 1024 bytes. The blocks are called SCREENS because each can be displayed as sixteen 64-character lines on a video display device. This philosophy permits any screen on a diskette to be read or written with one access.

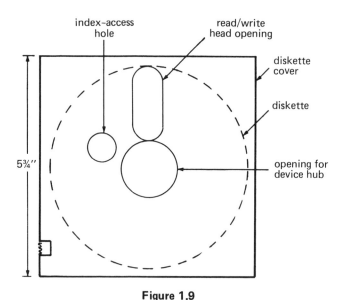

Figure 1.9
Typical diskette

VOCABULARY

A general familiarity with the following terms will help in learning computer fundamentals:

Accumulator
Arithmetic/logic unit
Bandwidth
Bus
Control unit

Diskette
Disk pack
Disk storage
Disk volume
Dynamic RAM
Erasable programmable read-only memory (EPROM)
Execution cycle (I-cycle)
Firmware
Floppy disk
General-purpose registers
Hard-sector disk
Harvard architecture
Hardware
Index register
Instruction cycle (I-cycle)
Instruction register
Memory-address register
Memory-data register
Memory refresh register
Microcomputer
Microprocessor
Princeton architecture
Program counter
Programmable read-only memory (PROM)
Random-access memory (RAM)
Read-only memory (ROM)
Register
Screen
Sector
Soft disk
Soft-sector disk
Software
Stack
Stack pointer
Static RAM
von Neumann machine
Winchester disk

EXERCISES

1. List a couple of items normally treated as "black boxes."

2.   Does a modern programmable calculator adhere to the Harvard or Princeton architecture?

3.   Some computer engineers refer to "read write" memory. Would that be ROM or RAM?

4.   Create a scenario wherein bandwidth would contribute to less than optimal performance.

5.   What common computer functions would be described by the following procedures:

    (a) Place address in memory address
        register (MAR)
     Issue read command
     Take word from memory data register
      (MDR)

    (b) Place address in memory address
        register (MAR)
     Place word in memory data register
      (MDR)
     Issue write command

Chapter 2. SOFTWARE TECHNOLOGY

Computer software can be viewed collectively as the set of instructions necessary for using the computer. However, the concept is not as well-defined as one might imagine. Some people view software as only those elements that "go with" the machine. Anything that deals with the user's applications, therefore, would be outside the scope of software and known as "application programs." Other people view software in the collective sense to include "all of the above." Regardless of one's point of view, software is a more tractable medium than hardware and much of the power of modern computers is available through effective software. As an example, the FORTH language is available to the user as an element of software.

REASONS FOR USING SOFTWARE

Software is one of the most popular topics in the computer field. This is so for a variety of reasons. First, a software program is the key interface in most cases between a person and a computer. Through the use of appropriate software, almost anyone can use a computer. Without software, specific technical training is needed to use a computer. Second, programming languages and operational software make it relatively straightforward to do programming so that the time and costs necessary for program development are decreased. Third, the use of a machine-independent programming language allows a program to be run on several computers. Lastly, software permits the computer to be used efficiently and effectively, and permits a computer system to be tailored to a particular application domain.

CATEGORIES OF SOFTWARE

Computer software is conveniently grouped into four major classes for the purposes of this book: programming languages, language processors, monitors and operating systems, and utility systems. A fifth class, "Data Management and Database Systems," is also recognized. This class is outside the scope of the FORTH language and is not covered further. Another software related topic is "Development Systems," which is also briefly discussed in this chapter.

PROGRAMMING LANGUAGES include assembler language and higher-level languages. FORTH is a higher-level language. LANGUAGE PROCESSORS include assemblers, compilers, and interpreters. Programming languages are available to the user through language processors. MONITORS AND OPERATING SYSTEMS are the set of routines that control the operation of the computer through facilities for system management, program management, and data management. Closely related to the previous category are UTILITY SYSTEMS, which supply the capacity for editing and debugging programs.

DEVELOPMENT SYSTEMS permit a program to be prepared and tested on one microcomputer system for use on a distinct system. Many typical applications of microprocessors and microcomputers require a development system because the application itself does not involve a complete computer system.

THE CONCEPT OF AN ALGORITHM

Generally speaking, an ALGORITHM is a set of procedures to be followed in solving any problem of a given kind. Procedures of this kind can be specified in a variety of ways ranging from concise mathematical formulation to description in a natural language, such as English. For example, a mathematical algorithm for computing the square root r of a number x is given as follows (where e is a small value):

STEP	INSTRUCTION
1	Set r equal to 1
2	Compute $r=.5(x/r+r)$
3	If $\lvert (r-x) \rvert < e$, then r is the desired result; otherwise go to step 2

Similarly, a less formal algorithm for computing the greatest common divisor of two nonzero integers A and B is given as follows:

1. Compare the numbers A and B; if they are equal, then each is the desired result.

2. If B is larger than A, exchange their values so that A always contains the larger value.

3. Compute A-B and replace A with the result. Continue with step 1.

From these examples, an idea of the characteristics of an algorithm can be determined:

THE DETERMINISTIC NATURE OF AN ALGORITHM. An algorithm must be given in the form of a finite list of instructions giving the exact procedure to be followed at each step of the calculation. Thus, the calculation does not depend on the calculator; it is a deterministic process that can be repeated successfully at any time and by anyone.

THE GENERALITY OF AN ALGORITHM. An algorithm is a single list of instructions defining a calculation which may be carried out on any initial data and which, in each case, gives the correct result. In other words, an algorithm tells how to solve not just one particular problem, but a whole class of similar problems.

In spite of the specificity of an algorithm, it can also be seen that the actual number of instructions that must be executed in solving a particular problem is not known beforehand, and is dependent upon the input data. The number is discovered only during the course of computation.

THE CONCEPT OF A PROGRAM

One of the most straightforward definitions of programming was given in 1958 by John von Neumann [21]:

> "... any computing machine that is to solve a complex mathematical problem must be 'programmed' for this task. This means that the complex operation of solving that problem must be replaced by a combination of the basic operations of the machine."

A COMPUTER PROGRAM (usually referred to simply as a PROGRAM) is a series of statements that specifies a computer representation of an algorithmic process. When the statements are executed, the algorithm is performed. The "statements" are the key entity and always adhere to the specifications for a given programming language.

Informally, a statement is a series of characters punched on a card, recorded on disk or tape, or entered at a terminal or display device. To be useful, however, a given statement must adhere to the SYNTAX (rules) and utilize the SEMANTICS (operational meaning) of the language being used. Some examples of languages and programs are included in the following sections.

ASSEMBLER LANGUAGE

Assembler language is closely related to the machine language of the computer: operation codes,

operands, and modifiers are simply represented by
symbolic   equivalents.   Consider   the assembler
language   program (listed as Figure 2.1) that
computes the greatest common divisor of numbers A
and B, as described above.   Each statement is
written according to a format consisting of a
"location" field, an "operation code" field, an
"operand"   feld, and a "comments" field.   The
LOCATION   FIELD   is   used   to reference the
corresponding machine instruction or data field.
The contents of the OPERATION CODE and OPERAND
fields are used to construct machine instructions,
to establish storage areas, and to specify program
constants.   Assembler language is not generally
considered to be a higher-level language, so that a
program written in assembler language is not as
readable as one written in a modern programming
language such as BASIC or FORTRAN. As a language,
FORTH is more readable than assembler language, but
probably not as readable - at least to the beginner
- as some other programming languages.

                PROGRAMMING LANGUAGES

     As an example of a program in a programming
language, consider the BASIC program in Figure 2.2
that computes the greatest common divisor, as
introduced in the previous algorithm and assembler
language program.   Each statement is identified by
a line number that is followed by a statement that
performs a computer function. Even though you may
not be familiar with the BASIC language, it is
still possible to follow the flow of the program
segment by referring to the algorithm. Similarly,
the FORTRAN program in Figure 2.3 computes the
square   root   of x.   Also, by following the
algorithm, this program is reasonably easy to
comprehend.   The essence of programming languages
is readability, writeability, and efficiency.
     FORTH is a programming language and several
examples of how it is used were given in the first
chapter.   FORTH and other popular programming

Location	Operation Code	Operand	Comments
REPEAT	L	5,A	Load register 5 with A.
	C	5,B	Compare reg. 5 (i.e., A) with B.
	BE	DONE	Branch if equal to DONE.
	BH	OK	Branch if reg. 5 (i.e., A) is greater than B to OK
	LR	6,5	Exchange A and B by placing A in register 6, by
	L	5,B	loading reg. 5 with B and then by placing the
	ST	6,B	contents of reg. 6 (i.e., the old A) in B.
OK	S	5,B	Subtract B from A.
	B	REPEAT	Branch to locate REPEAT to continue algorithm.
DONE	.		(Program would continue here.)
	.		
A	DS	F	Storage for A.
B	DS	F	Storage for B.

Figure 2.1
**Assembler language program segment to compute the greatest
common divisor of A and B**

```
10   IF A=B THEN GOTO 80
20   IF A>B THEN GOTO 60
30   T=A
40   A=B
50   B=T
60   A=A-B
70   GOTO 10
80   (continuation of program)
```

Figure 2.2
A BASIC program segment that computes the greatest
common divisor of A and B.

```
     E=.001
     R=1.0
2    R=.5*(X/R-R).GE.E) GOTO 2
     (continuation of program)
```

Figure 2.3
A FORTRAN program segment that computes
the square root of x.

languages in this category are designed primarily
to aid in the preparation of computer programs for
subsequent execution on a digital computer. These
languages are normally referred to as
"higher-level" or "procedure-oriented" languages.
The implications are twofold: (1) A program can be
written in one of these languages without the user
necessarily knowing the specific details of the
particular computer on which the program is to be
run; and (2) When writing a program in one of these
languages, the user describes the steps to be
performed by the computer as compared to a case in

which a language is used to describe the problem to be solved.

While a user must state the steps to be followed in the execution of the computer program, many of the details ordinarily associated with "machine-level" programming are eliminated. The significance of the preceding concepts is demonstrated in the following program, written in the BASIC language, that computes a table of even numbers less than or equal to 100 and their squares:

```
10  FOR I=2 TO 100 STEP 2
20  PRINT I, I 2
30  NEXT I
99  END
```

The statement numbered 10 marks the beginning of a series of statements that are to be executed repetitively while "I" successively takes on the values 2,4,6,...,100. The statement numbered 20 specifies that the values "I" and "I squared" should be printed on the same line. In the case of "I squared," a numerical calculation is required through the use of the operator, which represents exponentiation. The statement numbered 30 specifies that the loop should be repeated for the next value of I. Lastly, statement numbered 99 ends the program. When the program is executed, a single line is printed for each trip through the loop. The output would look somewhat as follows:

```
 2      4
 4     16
 6     36
 8     64
10    100
```

and so forth.

Some of the other well known programming languages and their major applications are:

FORTRAN for scientific computing

COBOL for data processing
Pascal for general programming

In fact a Pascal program for the "I squared" program is given as Figure 2.4. Pascal appears to be more complicated than BASIC or FORTRAN, but the difference is only superficial. In fact, the structure of the Pascal language makes it easier to write correct programs. The same philosophy would apply to FORTH. The language demands an investment in learning but the result is certainly worthwhile in terms of efficiency and flexibility.

```
PROGRAM TABLE(INPUT, OUTPUT);
  VAR
    I:
      INTEGER;
  BEGIN
    FOR I := 1 TO 50 DO
      WRITELN(2*I,SQR(2*I))
  END.
```

Figure 2.4
A Pascal program that computes a table of "I" and "I squared."

Each programming language is designed with a specific purpose in mind. The FORTH language is particularly suited for the programming of microcomputers.

PROGRAM STRUCTURE

Statements in a program are executed sequentially until a statement is executed that alters the normal sequence. The IF and GOTO statements, in previous examples, were statements in this category.

Most computer programs are designed so that

certain operational functions, such as the square root, are repeated frequently in the execution of the program. Thus, the machine instructions necessary for computing the square root (in this case) would be duplicated many times - an inefficient means of using valuable RAM memory. An alternate method and the one that is most frequently used is to include the square root function in the program only once as a "subprogram" and branch to it when needed. The process of using a "subprogram" is depicted conceptually in Figure 2.5. Thus, a program is effectively structured into a MAIN PROGRAM and possibly one or more SUBPROGRAMS.   A main program can reference subprograms, a subprogram can reference other subprograms, and so forth.

A subprogram is roughly equivalent to the definition mode in FORTH. This is how programs are synthesized in FORTH: as successive layers of subprograms.

LANGUAGE PROCESSORS

One of the key factors in the widespread use of programming languages is the fact that much of the detail ordinarily associated with "machine-level" programming is subordinated to another computer program, termed a "language processor." More specifically, a LANGUAGE PROCESSOR is a program that accepts another program as input; the output of a language processor either is a translated version of the input program or a set of computed results.

A LANGUAGE TRANSLATOR is a language processor that produces an output program. Some terminology relevant to the use of language translators is shown in Figure 2.6. The program as expressed in assembler language or in a higher-level language is referred to as a SOURCE PROGRAM; it is read into the language translator from cards, tape, a direct-access device, or from a terminal or display device. The output from the language translator is

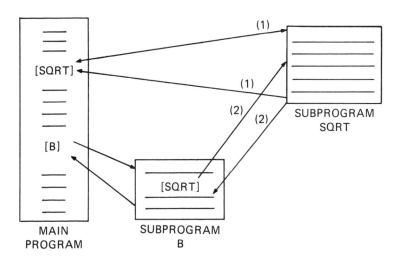

Figure 2.5
Conceptual view of the process of structuring a program into a
main program and one or more subprograms

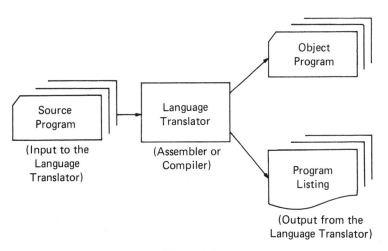

Figure 2.6
Conceptual view of the process of language translation.

a translated version of the program, termed an OBJECT PROGRAM, and a listing of the program. The object program is recorded on cards, tape, or a direct-access device for subsequent input to the computer for execution. Language translators come in two forms: assemblers and compilers.

ASSEMBLER PROGRAMS

An ASSEMBLER PROGRAM (usually referred to simply as an ASSEMBLER) converts a program written in assembler language to an equivalent program in machine language. The translation process is usually referred to as ASSEMBLY or the ASSEMBLY PROCESS. Assembly is usually performed in two passes over a source program. In the first pass, relative addresses are assigned to symbols in the location field. In the second pass over the source program, symbolic operation codes are replaced by internal machine codes and symbolic operands are replaced by corresponding addresses that were determined during pass one. The object program and the program listing are also produced during pass two. Various forms of error checking and analysis are performed during both passes.

COMPILER PROGRAMS

A COMPILER PROGRAM (usually referred to simply as a COMPILER) converts a program written in a higher-level language to either machine language or to assembler language. In the second case, the resulting assembler language program must then be processed by the assembler. Figure 2.7 depicts sample assembler language statements that would be generated by a single statement in a higher-level language.

HIGHER-LEVEL   ASSEMBLER LANGUAGE
   LANGUAGE

I=J*K+L   L   6,J (Load 6 with J)
                     M   5,K (Mult.regs. 5-6 by K)
                     A   6,L (Add L to reg. 6)
                     ST   6,I (Store reg. 6 in I)

Figure 2.7   Sample assembler language statements
             generated by a compiler.

In contradistinction to assembly where one machine
instruction is usually generated for each assembler
language source statement, the compiler usually
generates several machine instructions for each
source statement in a higher-level language.
Compilation is generally considered to be more
complicated than assembly since higher-level
language structure tends to be more complex than
assembler language structure. Although a compiler
is necessarily dependent on the language being
compiled, the following steps are usually involved:

   1. The compiler reads the source program on a
   statement-by-statement basis and performs the
   following processing for each statement:

      (a) Lexical analysis to identify keywords,
      names, constants, punctuation characters,
      etc.

      (b) Syntactical analysis to identify the
      type of statement and determine that its
      structure is admissible

      (c) Placing the constituents of the
      statement in lists and tables to facilitate
      the generation of machine code and to allow
      a global analysis of the program.

   2. A flow analysis of the program is performed
   to check for interstatement errors and to

provide information on how machine registers should be assigned.

3. Program optimization is performed and machine instructions are generated.

4. An object program and a program listing are produced.

A compiler and an assembler have one important feature in common. That is, each has the complete source program at its disposal so that the various steps in the assembly and compilation processes can be executed at the discretion of the person designing the assembler or the compiler. Only after a source program has been completely analyzed by an assembler or compiler and an object program produced is that object program actually executed.

INTERPRETER PROGRAMS

One type of language processor that allows program modification during execution is the interpreter. The INTERPRETER is a language processor that executes a source program without producing an object program. An interpreter operates as follows:

1. The interpreter reads the source program on a statement-by-statement basis and performs the following processing for each statement:

   (a) The statement is scanned, identified, analyzed, and interpreted to determine he operations that should be performed.

   (b) The required operations are executed by the interpreter and the intermediate results are retained.

2. The next statement that is interpreted depends on the results of the statement just

executed   (such   as   in   the   case   of   a   GOTO
statement).

Interpreters   vary   in   internal   design.   Some
interpreters   convert   a   source   program   into   an
intermediate   function   language   and   then
interpretively   execute   the   statements   in   the
intermediate   form.   The key point is that an object
program   is not produced and that all statements are
not necessarily processed by the interpreter.

Interestingly   enough, the FORTH concept employs
both   a   compiler   and   an   interpreter.   Statements
entered   in the definition mode are compiled into an
internal   form.   In the execution mode, statements
are then handled interpretively.

MONITORS AND OPERATING SYSTEMS

The   title   "monitors   and   operating   systems"
refers   to   a   set   of systems programs that provide
three major functions:

1. A logical interface between the hardware and
the software

2. A logical interface between the user and the
software

3. A   logical   interface   between   the user and
data   stored on "external" storage devices, such
as tape or diskette

If   the   set   of   systems programs are stored in ROM
and   only   ROM,   then   it   is   called a MONITOR that
normally   controls   the   execution   of all programs.
Moreover,   all   programs   use   the   monitor   during
execution.   Typical monitor capabilities are:

1. Automatic startup from ROM

2.   Handling   standard input from the keyboard
and output to the video display

3.   Examining, changing, moving, and comparing the contents of memory

4.   Examining and changing the contents of registers

5.   Saving the contents of memory on tape and reading the contents of memory from tape

6. Running and listing programs

7. Loading and saving programs from tape

Monitors are normally associated with reasonably small microcomputer systems that utilize tape cassettes for storing programs and data.
    When the set of systems programs are stored on disk storage and utilize a disk or diskette for storing programs and data, then it is called an OPERATING SYSTEM.   Like a monitor, an operating system controls the execution of all programs, and all programs use the operating system during execution.   Typical operating system capabilities are classed into three categories: program management, data management, and user services. PROGRAM MANAGEMENT facilities concern the following functions:

1. Loading programs from disk

2. Running programs from disk

3. Saving programs on disk

DATA MANAGEMENT facilities involve the following:

1. Storing data files and programs on disk by name

2. Copying files

3. Erasing files from disk

4. Renaming files

5. Providing disk input/output operations

USER SERVICE facilities involve the following:

1. Managing the catalog of program and data file names

2. Initializing disk

3. Establishing system parameters

In disk based microcomputers, both monitor and operating system facilities are commonly available to the user, providing the convenience of a ROM based system with the power of a disk operating system.

UTILITY SYSTEMS

Two software elements are available in most computer systems to aid the user in writing and debugging programs: an editor and a debug package. An EDITOR is a text processing system that permits a program to be entered into the system, changed, and listed with a minimum of inconvenience. Once the program file is constructed, editor commands permit textual modifications to be made to the program text at the statement level without requiring that the user re-enter a complete program line.
    A DEBUG PACKAGE assists the user in correcting program errors by supplying a means of tracing program flow and displaying intermediate results on a conditional basis.
    Editors and debug packages are commonly regarded as part of the operational environment for program development.

DEVELOPMENT SYSTEMS

Many microcomputer systems cannot support the program development process. A microcomputer system in an automobile, appliance, or other machine is relatively limited in functional capability because of the specialized nature of the application. Some of the necessary hardware elements (such as large RAM memory, printer, tape, or disk) simply do not exist. In cases such as this, programs are developed on a "development system" and then transferred to the specialized system.

There is nothing special about a development system, other than the fact that it can support the program development process through the following hardware and software elements (see Figure 2.8):

o Editor
o Debug package
o Language processor
o Monitor or operating system
o Printer
o Tape or disk storage
o Sufficiently large RAM

Each of these elements has been presented previously.

A development system need not be the same model of computer as the target system. Frequently, mini or large-scale computers are used to develop a program for a microcomputer system. When assembly is done on one computer (i.e., a development system) for another computer (usually a microcomputer), the language processor is called a CROSS ASSEMBLER. Similarly, compilation on one system for another computer is called a CROSS COMPILER.

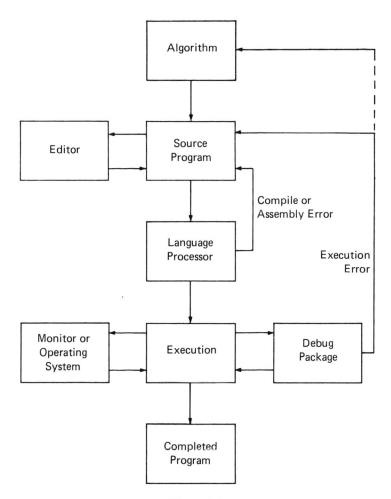

Figure 2.8
The program development process

VOCABULARY

A general familiarity with the following terms will help in understanding software technology:

Algorithm
Assembler language
Assembler program
Compiler program
Cross assembler
Cross compiler
Debug package
Development system
Editor
Higher-level language
Interpreter program
Language processor
Language translator
Main program
Monitor
Operating system
Procedure-oriented language
Program
Programming language
Subprogram
Utility system

EXERCISES

1. What do an algorithm and an ordinary kitchen recipe have in common?

2. How many steps are in the greatest common divisor algorithm given in the chapter? Apply this algorithm to the values 35 and 21. How many steps are actually executed?

3. Name the fields in an assembler language statement.

4. Give the output from a language translator. Give the output from an interpreter.

Chapter 3. REVERSE POLISH NOTATION

Mathematical Forms

Structure of Expressions

Conversion Between Infix Notation and
  Postfix Notation

Interpretive Execution of Infix Notation

Vocabulary

Exercises

A good working knowledge of the FORTH language
requires that a user have a good background in
reverse Polish notation and the use of a stack.
Both topics have been introduced previously. This
chapter goes into more detail so that a user can
easily convert expressions to reverse Polish
notation and understand how they are executed in
FORTH. Clearly, a user can do simple things in
FORTH without possessing any special knowledge. As
the level of complication increases, however,
background information is important for effective
programming. This chapter does not have any
specific orientation to FORTH or any other
programming language. The subject matter is simply
presented to assist the programmer whenever needed.

MATHEMATICAL FORMS

Ordinary mathematical notation is referred to
as INFIX NOTATION, which means that the operator
symbol for an operation requiring two operands
separates the operands. Examples of infix notation
are: x+y, which means "add the value of y to the
value of x," and -a, which means "take the negative
of a." When an expression includes more than one
operation, then an operational convention is used
to determine the order in which the operations are
executed. The most widely used convention is to
establish a hierarchy among operators, such as the
following:

OPERATOR SYMBOL	HIERARCHY	OPERATIONAL MEANING
**	High	Exponentiation
* or /		Multiplication or division
+ or -	Low	Addition or subtraction

and then to execute operators by order of
hierarchy. Thus, an expression such as

$$\frac{a}{x+y}$$

requires the use of parentheses, that is

$$A/(X+Y)$$

to specify the intended meaning.

A notation that does not require parentheses for expressions of this sort is called Polish notation, after the Polish mathematician J. Lukasewicz, who used it for representing well-formed formulas in logic. In fact, Polish notation never requires parentheses and is known as a "parenthesis-free" notation. Polish notation comes in two varieties: PREFIX NOTATION, which is also called simply Polish notation; and POSTFIX NOTATION, which is also called reverse Polish notation. In prefix notation, the operator always precedes its operands (reading from left to right), so that an expression such as A+B is denoted by +AB. More complex expressions are constructed by repeated application of the concept in a similar manner. Additional examples of mathematical expressions represented in prefix notation are given in Table 3.1.

Table 3.1

Examples of Polish Notation

Infix Notation	Prefix Notation	Postfix Notation
A*B	*AB	AB*
A*X-B	-*AXB	AX*B-
A*(X-B)	*A-XB	AXB-*
A+(B/C-D)	+A-/BCD	ABC/D-+
A*(B/(C-D)+E)	*A+/B-CDE	ABCD-/E+*

POSTFIX NOTATION is the most popular form of Polish notation and is characterized by the fact that the operands precede the operator (again reading from left to right), so that the infix expression A+B is represented by AB+. Additional examples of postfix notation are given in Table 3.1. The major advantages of postfix notation are inherent in the relative simplicity of the processes required to: (1) convert an expression from infix notation to postfix notation; and (2) execute the postfix notation interpretively or convert it to a set of equivalent machine language instructions. A description of the conversion process from infix notation to postfix notation is given in a subsequent paragraph.

STRUCTURE OF EXPRESSIONS

One means of showing the relationship between operators and operands in an expression and exhibiting the order in which operations should be executed is to use a STRUCTURAL DIAGRAM. In a diagram of this type, operators and operands are regarded as points (or nodes), and the relationship between them is denoted by lines, as shown in Figure 3.1. A structural diagram provides two important items of information about an expression: (1) its form, and (2) its structural meaning. In general, a structural diagram is independent of the syntactic structure of a programming language.

A structural diagram can be regarded as an upside-down tree. The topmost node is the "root" and operands are always terminal nodes or "leaves" of the tree. Another way to look at a structural diagram is to view it as a hierarchical collection of subtrees, where each operator is the root of a subtree and the operands (to that operator) are leaves of that subtree. Thus, an operator is always the root of a subtree. A binary operator has two subtrees, corresponding to each of its operands. A unary operator has a single subtree, corresponding to its single operand. Figure 3.2

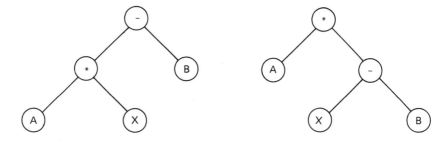

(A) Structure diagram for A*X–B   (B) Structure diagram for A*(X–B)

Figure 3.1
Structure diagrams used to exhibit the relationship between operators
and operands in an expression.

(A) Representation of a binary operator   (B) Representation of a unary operator

Figure 3.2
Structural forms for binary and unary operators.

gives   structural   forms   for   binary   and   unary
operators.

Trees (or structural diagrams) do   not   lend
themselves to representation in the computer, for
obvious   reasons, and are stored as a linear
sequence of symbols.   The process of converting a
tree   to   a   linear   sequence   of   symbols   is
accomplished by traversing (or walking through) the
tree.   Knuth [14] defines three methods that are
applied by systematically dividing a tree into
subtrees.   The three methods (modified to meet our
needs) are given as:

PREORDER TRAVERSAL

Visit the root
Traverse the left subtree
Traverse the right subtree
or
Visit the root
Traverse the single subtree

POSTORDER TRAVERSAL

Traverse the left subtree
Visit the root
Traverse the right subtree
or
Visit the root
Traverse the single subtree

ENDORDER TRAVERSAL

Traverse the left subtree
Traverse the right subtree
Visit the root
or
Traverse the single subtree
Visit the root

The three forms of traversal are depicted in Figure
3.3.   Figure 3.4 gives additional examples, of
which the last includes unary operators.
    An interesting relationship exists between the
structural diagram (or tree form) of an expression
and infix, prefix, and postfix notation. If the
"tree of an expression" is denoted by TOE, then

        PREORDER (TOE) - prefix notation
        ENDORDER (TOE) - postfix notation
        POSTORDER (TOE) - infix notation without
                            parentheses

In the last case, the relationship has validity
only for expressions without parentheses, but is a
useful conceptual tool.   As an example of these
concepts, consider the tree named Q in Figure 3.5.
Application of the three forms of traversal gives

        PREORDER(Q)   =A+*BC/DE, which is prefix
                        notation
        POSTORDER   A=B*C*D/E, which is infix notation
        ENDORDER(Q)   ABC*DE/+=, which is postfix
                        notation

    This last example incorporates the conventional
replacement operation of the form

                        v=e

where v is a variable and e is an expression. This
can be regarded as a binary operation that takes
the form =ve in prefix notation and ve= in postfix
notation.
    It should be emphasized here that another symbol
is used for the "store" operation in FORTH. If it
were desired to replace the contents of variable A

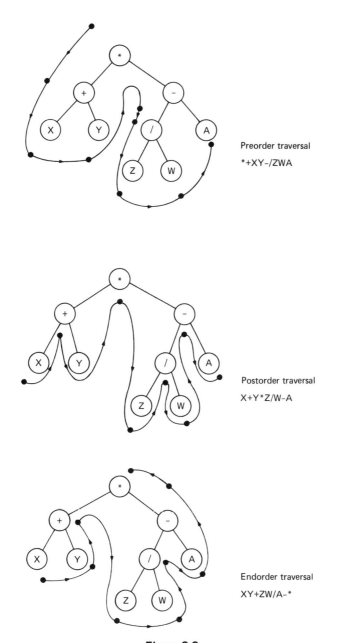

Preorder traversal

*+XY-/ZWA

Postorder traversal

X+Y*Z/W-A

Endorder traversal

XY+ZW/A-*

Figure 3.3
Preorder, postorder, and endorder traversal of the structural diagram
of the expression (X+Y) *Z/W-A).

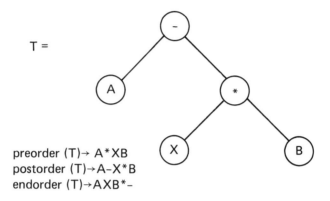

T =

preorder (T)→ A*XB
postorder (T)→A-X*B
endorder (T)→AXB*-

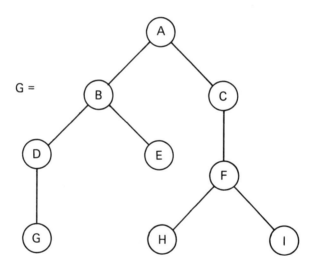

G =

preorder (G)→ABDGECFHI
postorder (G)→DGBEACHFI
endorder (G)→GDEBHIFCA

Figure 3.4
Examples of preorder, postorder, and endorder traversal.

with the value 5 in FORTH, one would enter:

5 A !

where {!} represents the store operation.

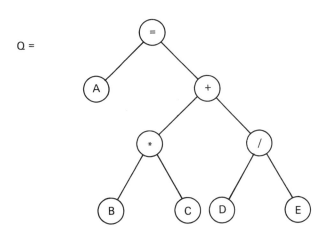

Q =

Figure 3.5
Structural diagram of the statement A=B*C+D/E. This example is used
in the text to show the relationship between traversal and
mathematical forms.

CONVERSION BETWEEN INFIX NOTATION AND POSTFIX NOTATION

The conversion process from infix notation to postfix notation is given here as a basic method that a user can apply to complex expressions. The description of the method utilizes operands that are single letters and does not permit subscripted variables. Methods for interpretively executing postfix notation follow this section.

Conversion from infix notation to postfix notation uses a set of procedures and a hierarchy (or priority) among operators. The overall process is depicted in Figure 3.6. The terms SOURCE STRING

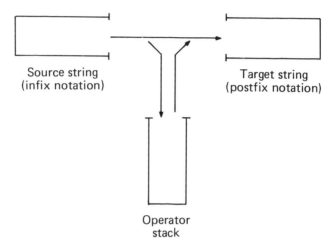

Figure 3.6
Basic diagram of the conversion process from infix and postfix notation.

and TARGET STRING are particularly appropriate because the expression can be regarded as a string of characters. After conversion from infix to postfix notation, the order of operands (that is, variables) remains the same. During conversion, an OPERATOR STACK is used to rearrange the operators so that they occur in the target string in the order in which they should be executed. The priority of operators is as follows:

PRIORITY	OPERATOR OR SYMBOL	NOTE
High	(	Outside the operator stack
	* or /	
	+ or -	
Low	(	Inside the operator stack

A small subset of operators, including parentheses,
is selected to simplify the conversion process.
Rules for manipulating the source and target
strings and the operator stack can now be given:

1. The source string is scanned from left to
right. Similarly, the target string is formed
from left to right.

2. Operands (that is, variables) from the
source string bypass the operator stack and are
passed to the target string directly.

3. If the scan of the source string encounters
an operator with a priority greater than the
priority of the operator at the top of the
operator stack, then the operator from the
source string is entered into the operator
stack. If the priority of the operator in the
source string is not greater than the priority
of the operator at the top of the operator
stack, then the operator at the top of the
operator stack is moved to the target string
and this step is repeated. (Note: a left
parenthesis always enters the operator stack.)

4. If a right parenthesis is encountered during
the scan of the source string, then the
operators in the operator stack are moved to
the target string. This process continues
until a left parenthesis is encountered in the
operator stack; then the left and right
parentheses are both discarded.

5. When the end of the source string is
reached, all operators in the operator stack
are moved directly to the target string.

Figure 3.7 gives a detailed "walk-through" of the
conversion process using the above rules and
operator priorities.

Source String	Operator Stack	Target String
↑A+B*C−D)/E		
↑+(B*C−D)/E		A
↑(B*C−D)/E	+	A
↑B*C−D)/E	(+	A
↑*C−D)/E	(+	AB
↑C−D)/E	* (+	AB
↑−D)/E	* (+	ABC
↑D)/E	− (+	ABC*
↑)/E	− (+	ABC*D
↑/E	+	ABC*D−
↑E	/ +	ABC*D−
↑	/ +	ABC*D−E
(↑ Denotes scan pointer)		ABC*D−E/+

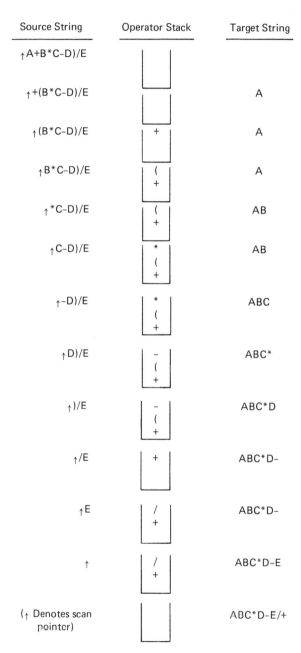

Figure 3.7
Conversion from infix notation to postfix notation.

INTERPRETIVE EXECUTION OF INFIX NOTATION

Interpretive execution of an expression in postfix notation involves a left-to-right scan and the use of an operand stack. If an operand is encountered during the scan, its value is placed in the operand stack. If an operator is encountered during the scan, the required number of values (i.e., two operands for binary operators and one operand for unary operators) are taken from the operand stack. The specified operation is performed on the operand(s) and the result is placed back in the stack. An example of interpretive execution is given in Figure 3.8. When the process is complete, the computed value of the expression is at the top of the operand stack.

In FORTH, placing the value of a variable in the stack is not as straightforward as the above examples might imply. If a user wished to compute A+5, for example, and entered the following FORTH input line:

5 A +

the "address" of A would be added to 5, since a variable reference puts the address of a variable in the stack in the FORTH language. The following input line:

5 A @ +

would be needed to add the contents of A to 5. The symbol {@} is a FORTH word that fetches the contents of the address on the top of the stack and pushes the value into the stack.

Postfix String	Operand Stack	Note
XY+ZW/A-B+Y/	(empty)	Prior to scan of postfix string; stack empty
Y+ZW/A-*B+Y/	2	Value of X is pushed into stack
+ZW/A-*B+Y/	3 2	Value of Y is pushed into stack
ZW/A-*B+Y/	5	+ operator; two operands (3 and 2) are pulled from top of stack operation is performed on them; result is pushed into stack
W/A-*B+Y/	12 5	Value of Z is pushed into stack
/A-*B+Y/	4 12 5	Value of W is pushed into stack
A-*B+Y/	3 5	/ operator; two operands (4 and 12) are pulled from top of stack; operation is performed on them; result is pushed into stack
-*B+Y/	1 3 5	Value of A is pushed into stack
*B+Y/	2 5	- operator; two operands (1 and 3) are pulled from top of stack; operation is performed on them; result is pushed into stack
B+Y/	10	* operator; two operands (2 and 5) are pulled from top of stack; operation is performed on them; result is pushed into stack
+Y/	5 10	Value of B is pushed into stack
Y/	15	+ operator; two operands (5 and 10) are pulled from top of stack; operation is performed on them; result is pushed into stack
/	3 15	Value of Y is pushed into stack
	5	/ operator; two operands (3 and 15) are pulled from top of stack; operation is performed on them; result is pushed into
	5	Execution of postfix string is complete; result is in the operand stack

Value of Operands

Symbol	Value
X	2
Y	3
Z	12
W	4
A	1
B	5

Figure 3.8
Interpretive execution of the postfix expression XY+ZW/A-*B+Y/
that corresponds to the infix expression ((X+Y)*(Z/W-A)+B)/Y.

VOCABULARY

A general familiarity with the following terms will help in learning the concepts of reverse Polish notation:

Binary operator
Endorder traversal
Infix notation
Operator hierarchy
Postfix notation
Postorder traversal
Prefix notation
Preorder traversal
Structural diagram
Unary operator

EXERCISES

1. Convert the following expressions to postfix notation:

```
A+B-C
(A+B)*C
A*B-C/D+E
(A+B)/(C-D)-E
(A*Y+B)*Y+C
(A*(B+C)-D)*E
((A*Y+B)*Y+C)*Y+D
```

2. Draw structural diagrams for the following:

```
A*B-C/D+E
(A*Y+B)*Y+C
```

3. Interpretively execute the following expressions in postfix notation:

```
ABC*-
ABC+*D-E*
```

AB*CD/-E+

using the following values:

VARIABLE	VALUE
A	10
B	2
C	4
D	5
E	3

4. Traverse the following tree

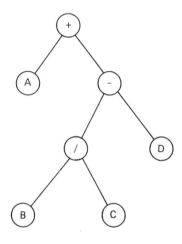

in preorder, postorder, and endorder form.

Chapter 4.   ELEMENTARY CALCULATIONS AND STACK
             MANIPULATION

FORTH Words

Punctuation

Looking at the Stack

Elementary Arithmetic Operations

Number Bases

Stack Manipulation Operations

Mathematical Functions

Complement Arithmetic

Vocabulary

Exercises

In order to do elementary calculations in FORTH, a person needs a knowledge of the command structure and the operational conventions of the system. While the FORTH system takes on the outward appearance of a calculator at the elementary level, the primary objective of the language is for conventional computer programming - especially at the microprocessor level - so that the language has considerably more expressive power than an ordinary calculator. It must be emphasized, however, that to some extent, FORTH capability is supported and also limited by the underlying hardware. This fact will become evident with regard to the data types and associated arithmetic operations that are available to the user via the FORTH language.

FORTH WORDS

Any symbol or sequence of characters that has meaning to the FORTH system is called a "word." So, for example, the symbol {+} and the word {DUP} are called FORTH WORDS. Recall here that items enclosed in braces are FORTH words. Normally the braces are used when the inclusion of a FORTH word in a sentence might cause confusion to the reader. The braces are also used for emphasis. There is no connection between a FORTH word and a computer word. In the latter case, a computer word is a hardware memory cell used to store an element of data.

In the first chapter, the stack was introduced as the place where numbers are held during computer operations. In this case, numbers include data values and also address values in the computer. FORTH words cannot be placed in the stack. In the execution mode, a FORTH statement is "generally" processed in the following manner:

o When a value is encountered, it is placed in the stack

o When a FORTH word is encountered, it is
executed

In the definition mode, numbers and words are
stored as part of the definition for subsequent
execution.

Some caution must be taken with punctuation
characters, such as {.} and {!}, which are in fact
FORTH words.   To FORTH, they are not punctuation
characters, but command the FORTH system to execute
the respective computer operation.   There are no
lexical restrictions on FORTH words. A FORTH word
can be composed of any character or group of
characters from the keyboard.

The concept of a word is so general in FORTH
that there is no need to specify the system's
character set.   Minimally, it can be expected to
include the letters (A through Z), digits (0
through 9), and a large selection of operators and
punctuation symbols, such as { + - * / . ! @ : ; "
' = > < ? ( ) , } .   Almost every symbol -
sometimes referred to as a special character in
other languages - has an operational meaning as a
FORTH word.

PUNCTUATION

There is one punctuation rule: FORTH WORDS MUST
BE SEPARATED BY AT LEAST ONE SPACE. This rule
stems from the need for visual fidelity and the
extreme lexigraphic generality of FORTH words.
Thus, a user may define any sequence of characters
as a FORTH word and it will not cause any confusion
to the FORTH system.

LOOKING AT THE STACK

It is frequently necessary to visualize the
stack in order to describe how a particular FORTH
operation works.   The FORTH convention for doing

this is to picture the stack as a series of tokens
with the top of the stack on the right and the
bottom of the stack on the left. Ordinary addition
can be used as an example. Recall that in
conventional mathematical notation, an addition
operation is expressed as "n1+n2" yielding the
result "sum;" you might write this as "n1+n2 sum,"
where the right arrow denotes "yields." Clearly,
in reverse Polish notation, the expression would be
represented as "n1 n2 + sum."

To visualize the stack, simply ignore the
operator symbol and picture only the stack. For
the above addition operation the stack would be
visualized as:

                        STACK
                Before   After

                n1 n2   sum

In this case, n2 is on the top of the stack because
it is on the right. The addition operation takes
the top two values from the stack and returns the
sum.

                ELEMENTARY ARITHMETIC OPERATIONS

        The elementary arithmetic operations in FORTH
and their respective operator symbols, recognized
as FORTH words, are:

        OPERATION   FORTH WORD

        Addition   +
        Subtraction   -
        Multiplication   *
        Division   /
        Modulus   MOD
        Divide Modulus   /MOD

These operations are defined on 16-bit integer
values that have a range of -32768 to +32767.

Double precision operations are covered in a separate chapter.

All arithmetic operations are defined on values held in the stack. It does not matter whether the values were placed in the stack directly or the values in the stack resulted from a previous FORTH operation. Terminology for the four basic arithmetic operations may be recalled as follows:

$$\begin{array}{cc}
\text{M (addend)} & \text{M (minuend)} \\
\underline{+\text{N (augend)}} & \underline{-\text{N (subtrahend)}} \\
\text{M+N (sum)} & \text{M-N (difference)}
\end{array}$$

$$\begin{array}{cc}
\text{M (multiplier)} & \text{M (dividend)} \\
\underline{*\text{M (multiplicand)}} & \underline{/\text{N (divisor)}} \\
\text{M*N (product)} & \text{M/N (quotient)}
\end{array}$$

In ordinary arithmetic, the division operation yields a remainder, described as follows: "dividend = divisor * quotient + remainder."

The ADDITION operation in FORTH is described symbolically as:

$$n1 \quad n2 \quad + \longrightarrow sum$$

where "n1" is the addend and "n2" is the augend. When the word {+} is encountered by FORTH, it adds the top two values in the stack (i.e., n1+n2) removes them, and places the sum in the stack. The values can be placed in the stack directly or may result from a previous computation. The following examples demonstrate addition:

2 3 + . 5 OK

4 1 + 8 + . 13 OK

14 3 + 2 5 + + . 24 OK

Recall that the underline denotes what the user has
entered. The "OK" denotes that the computation was
performed successfully and that the system is ready
for additional input.
    The SUBTRACTION operation in FORTH is described
symbolically as:

$$n1 \ n2 \ - \longrightarrow difference$$

where "n1" is the minuend and "n2" is the
subtrahend. When the word {-} is encountered by
FORTH, it subtracts the value on the top of the
stack from the value below it (i.e., n1-n2),
removes them, and places the difference in the
stack. As with other FORTH operations, the values
can be placed in the stack directly or may result
from a previous computation. The following
examples demonstrate subtraction:

    5 3 - . 2 OK

    20 10 - 5 - . 5 OK

    8 5 - 16 10 - - . -3 OK

It is important to remember with subtraction that
the subtrahend is always on the top of the stack.
    The MULTIPLICATION operation in FORTH is
described symbolically as:

$$n1 \ n2 \ * \longrightarrow product$$

where "n1" is the multiplier and "n2" is the
multiplicand. When the word {*} is encountered by
FORTH, it multiplies the top two values in the
stack (i.e., n1*n2), removes them, and places the
product in the stack. The following examples
demonstrate multiplication:

    3 2 * . 6 OK

7 4 2 * * . 56 OK

6 5 * 3 -1 * * . -90 OK

Because the basic arithmetic operations in FORTH
are defined on 16-bit integer values, a value
outside of the range -32768 to 32767 can be
produced from the arithmetic operations. The value
will be correctly computed but may yield unexpected
results, because FORTH uses binary two's complement
notation for internal data values. This subject
will be covered later in two sections: complement
arithmetic and double precision arithmetic.
   The DIVISION operation in FORTH is described
symbolically as:

n1 n2 /——→quotient

where "n1" is the dividend and "n2" is the divisor.
When the word {/} is encountered by FORTH, it
divides the value on the top of the stack into the
value below it (i.e., n1/n2), removes them, and
places the integer quotient in the stack. Since
the operation is integer division, the remainder is
lost. The following examples demonstrate integer
division:

6 2 / . 3 OK

5 3 / . 1 OK

18 3 / 2 / . 3 OK

11 2 / 15 7 / . 2 OK

11 2 / 15 -7 / / . -2 OK

The mathematical sign of the quotient is the sign
that results from the division operation. Two

related operations, {MOD} and {/MOD} can be used to
obtain the remainder from integer division.
     The MODULUS operation in FORTH is described
symbolically as:

                    n1 n2 MOD →remainder

where "n1" is the dividend and "n2" is the divisor.
When the word {MOD} is encountered by FORTH, it
divides the value on the top of the stack into the
value below it (i.e., n1/n2), removes them, and
places the remainder in the stack. The following
examples demonstrate the modulus operation:

     <u>11 3 MOD . 2</u> OK

     <u>4 2 MOD . 0</u> OK

     <u>-11 3 MOD . -2</u> OK

The algebraic sign of the remainder always is the
same as the algebraic sign of the dividend.
     The DIVIDE-MODULUS operation in FORTH is
described symbolically as:

               n1 n2 /MOD →remainder quotient

where "n1" is the dividend and "n2" is the divisor.
When the word {/MOD} is encountered by FORTH, it
divides the value on the top of the stack into the
value below it (i.e., n1/n2), removes them, and
places the quotient on the top of the stack and the
remainder below it.   More specifically, FORTH
pushes the remainder into the stack and then pushes
the quotient into the stack so that the quotient is
on the top. The following examples demonstrate the
divide-modulus operation:

     <u>11 3 /MOD . . 3 2</u> OK

4 2 /MOD . . 2 0 OK

-11 3 /MOD . . -3 -2 OK

The mathematical sign of the quotient is the sign that results from the division operation; the arithmetic sign of the remainder is always the same as the arithmetic sign of the dividend.

NUMBER BASES

When FORTH comes up, the system automatically operates in the decimal system (i.e., base 10). What this means is that numbers can be entered in decimal and the results are displayed in decimal. A user may change the number system used for entry and display and thereby adapt the FORTH system to the needs of a particular application. The hexadecimal number system is built into FORTH and it may be invoked by entering the FORTH word {HEX}. With relative ease, the user may also define other number systems, such as octal or binary.

To change to the hexadecimal, the user simply enters the word HEX. demonstrated as follows:

12 OK

HEX OK

. C OK

To return to the decimal system, the user just enters the word DECIMAL, demonstrated as follows:

DECIMAL OK

1234 . 1234 OK

1234 HEX . 4D2 OK

4D2 DECIMAL . 1234 OK

Once a number system is entered, FORTH stays in that system until the number base is changed.
   A number system is defined through a colon definition that assigns a value to the system variable BASE, as follows:

: BINARY 2 BASE ! ;

Then, to put FORTH into the binary system, all the user has to do is to enter the word BINARY:

: BINARY 2 BASE ! ; OK

BINARY OK

11 10 + . 101 OK

Similarly, the octal system can be defined with an analogous statement:

: OCTAL 8 BASE ! ; OK

OCTAL OK

5 7 + . 14 OK

Once, several number bases are defined, it is possible to switch between them almost at will:

DECIMAL 12345 HEX . 3039 OK

DECIMAL 12345 OCTAL . 30071 OK

DECIMAL 12345 BINARY . 11000000111001   OK

DECIMAL OK

All internal calculations in FORTH are performed in the binary number system. The number bases, introduced above, only affect input and output.

STACK MANIPULATION OPERATIONS

The FORTH language permits the stack to be manipulated directly to facilitate the construction of programs. In many cases, a single stack manipulation operation can simplify a program and decrease its execution time.

Recall the method of visualizing the stack, given previously, wherein the item on the right denotes the top of the stack. For example, in the following list:

n1 n2 n3

"n3" denotes the top of the stack, "n2" represents the number directly below it, and "n1" denotes the third number down.

The stack manipulation operations in FORTH and their respective FORTH words are:

OPERATION	FORTH WORD
Duplicates the top value on the stack	DUP
Exchanges top two values in the stack	SWAP
Removes top value from the stack	DROP

Copies the second number in the stack and puts it on the top	OVER
Rotates the third number in the stack and puts it on the top	ROT
Rotates the top N stack entries	ROLL
Duplicates the top value on the stack only if it is non-zero	-DUP
Duplicates the top value on the stack only if it is non-zero (Same as -DUP)	?DUP
Copies the n1-th stack item to the top	PICK
Counts the number of items on the stack	DEPTH

These operations are defined on 16-bit integer values that have a range of -32768 to 32767. Corresponding stack manipulation operations exist for double precision values and are introduced in a separate chapter.

The DUP operation takes the top value on the stack, duplicates it, and pushes the duplicated value into the stack. The stack contents before and after the execution of the DUP operation are:

Operation: DUP

```
Stack before: n1 n2 n3
Stack after:  n1 n2 n3 n3
```

The SWAP operation exchanges the top two values on the stack without disturbing the other stack values. The stack contents before and after the execution of the SWAP operation are:

```
Operation:    SWAP
Stack before: n1 n2 n3
Stack after:  n1 n3 n2
```

The DROP operation removes the value on the top of the stack so that all of the values below it are moved up. The stack contents before and after the execution of the DROP operation are:

```
Operation:    DROP
Stack before: n1 n2 n3
Stack after:  n1 n2
```

The OVER operation takes the second number in the stack, duplicates it, and pushes the duplicated value into the stack. The stack contents before and after the execution of the OVER operation are:

```
Operation:    OVER
Stack before: n1 n2 n3
Stack after:  n1 n2 n3 n2
```

The ROT operation works with the top three values in the stack. The value that is third from the top is rotated to the top and the two values above it are pushed down. The stack contents before and after the execution of the ROT operation are:

```
     Operation:    ROT
     Stack before: n1 n2 n3
     Stack after:  n2 n3 n1
```

The ROLL operation is similar to the ROT operation, but uses the value on the top of the stack to determine the "depth" of the roll. The statement {3 ROLL} is the same as the ROT operation. The stack contents before and after the execution of the ROLL operation are:

```
     Operation:    ROLL
     Stack before: n1 ... n(i-1) ni n(i+1) ... nk n
     Stack after:  n1 ... n(i-1) n(i+1) ... nk ni
```

where $i=k-n+1$. The value on the top of the stack that determines the depth of the roll is removed.

The {-DUP} operation inspects the top value on the stack. If it is zero, then the {-DUP} operation does nothing. If it is non-zero, then FORTH takes the value on the top of the stack, duplicates it, and pushes the duplicated value into the stack. The stack contents before and after the {-DUP} operation are:

```
     Operation:    -DUP
     Stack before: n1 n2 n3
     Stack after:  n1 n2 n3 n3, if n3 is non-zero
     Stack after:  n1 n2 n3, if n3 is zero
```

The FORTH word {?DUP} is synonymous with {-DUP} and is pronounced "query dup." The meaning is that the top item on the stack is inspected and duplicated only if it is nonzero.

The PICK operation copies a stack entry to the top of the stack without disturbing the relative

order of the values. This operation uses the
number on the top of the stack to determine the
"depth" of the PICK operation. The statement {1
PICK} is the same as the DUP operation, and the
statement {2 PICK} is the same as the OVER
operation. The stack contents before and after the
execution of the PICK operation are:

    Operation: PICK
    Stack before: n1 ... n(i-1) ni n(i+1) ... nk n
    Stack after: n1 ... n(i-1) ni n(i+1) ... nk ni

where i=k-n+1.   The value on the top of the stack
that determines the depth of the PICK operation is
removed.
    The DEPTH operation counts the number of items
in the stack and pushes that value into the stack.
This operation is described symbolically as:

$$n1 \; n2 \; DEPTH \longrightarrow n1 \; n2 \; n$$

where "n" is the number of items in the stack and
"n1" and "n2" are residual values. After the DEPTH
operation is executed, the stack contains "n+1"
items.
    Figure 4.1 gives several examples of
single-precision stack manipulation operations.
The examples are routine cases to demonstrate the
manner in which the stack manipulation operations
function. The last two examples in Figure 4.1
perhaps need further clarification. The following
FORTH statement:

$$3 \; 4 \; DUP \; * \; SWAP \; DUP \; * \; + \; .$$

is a means of computing the expression (in ordinary
mathematical notation): (H*H)+(B*B). The leftmost
DUP operation copies the top stack item giving 3 4
4 and the succeeding {*} operation multiplies the
top two numbers giving 16. The SWAP operation
exchanges the top values giving 16 and 3. The

```
5 DUP . . 5 5  OK
7 3 SWAP . . 7 3  OK
1 8 DROP . 1  OK
4 9 OVER . . . 4 9 4  OK
-7 3 9 ROT . . . -7 9 3  OK
-17 23 6 10 4 ROLL . . . . -17 10 6 23  OK
-11 4 -DUP . . 4 4  OK
-11 0 -DUP . . 0 -11  OK
-17 23 6 10 4 PICK . . . . . -17 10 6 23 -17  OK
3 4 DUP * SWAP DUP * + . 25  OK
: SQR DUP * ;  OK
5 SQR . 25  OK
```

Figure 4.1
Examples of stack manipulation operations.

rightmost DUP operation again copies the top entry
in the stack giving 16 3 3 and the following {*}
multiplies the top two numbers giving 16 9. The
final {+} operation computes the sum of the top two
values on the stack, giving 25, and the final dot
displays the result of 25.

The following colon definition:

: SQR DUP * ;

is a procedure that "squares" the top value on the
stack, removing the value and depositing its
square. The procedure is straightforward; the top
value on the stack is duplicated and then
multiplied by itself.

MATHEMATICAL FUNCTIONS

A set of mathematical functions are included in
the FORTH language to increase the efficiency of
the system. The functions could be programmed
using colon definitions; however, the execution
speed would be greater than with the use of
built-in functions. The following functions are

defined on 16-bit integer values:

FUNCTION	FORTH WORD
Absolute value	ABS
Maximum	MAX
Minimum	MIN
Times divide	*/
Times divide modulus	*/MOD
Sign	+-

Double precision functions are covered in a separate chapter.
   All mathematical functions are defined on values held in the stack. It does not matter whether the values were placed on the stack directly or the values in the stack resulted from a previous FORTH operation.
   The ABSOLUTE VALUE function in FORTH is described symbolically as:

                n1 ABS   n2

where "n2" is a positive integer. When the word {ABS} is encountered by FORTH, it removes the top stack entry, computes its absolute value, and places the result in the stack. The following examples demonstrate the absolute value function:

    -17 ABS . 17 OK

    75 ABS . 75 OK

There is a related mathematical operation in FORTH that computes the two's complement of the top value in the stack. This operation, termed "minus" is covered in the following section on complement arithmetic.
   The MAXIMUM function in FORTH is described

symbolically as:

$$n1 \ n2 \ MAX \longrightarrow n3$$

where "n3" is the maximum of "n1" and "n2." More specifically, the MAX function removes the top two values from the stack, computes the value that is mathematically larger, and places the result in the stack. The following examples demonstrate the maximum function:

<u>10 5 MAX . 10</u> OK

<u>-9 63 MAX . 63</u> OK

<u>-34 -6 MAX . -6</u> OK

The MINIMUM function is FORTH is described symbolically as:

$$n1 \ n2 \ MIN \longrightarrow n3$$

where "n3" is the minimum of "n1" and "n2." More specifically, the MIN function removes the top two values from the stack, computes the value that is mathematically smaller, and places the result back in the stack. The following examples demonstrate the minimum function:

<u>10 5 MIN . 5</u> OK

<u>-9 63 MIN . -9</u> OK

<u>-34 -6 MIN . -34</u> OK

The TIMES DIVIDE function computes the value of the expression n1*n2/n3 and is described symbolically as:

n1 n2 n3 */—→quotient

When the word {*/} is encountered by FORTH, it removes the top three values from the stack and performs the computation of the function in the following order:

    1. "n1" is multiplied by "n2" and a double precision product is retained.

    2. The double precision product is divided by "n3" yielding the single precision quotient.

    3. The quotient is placed in the stack.

The remainder from the division operation is lost. The following examples demonstrate the times divide function:

      3 4 2 */ . 6 OK

      -7 5 4 */ . -8 OK

It should be noted that the times divide function is more accurate than the sequence {n1 n2 * n3 /} because of the double precision intermediate product.
    The TIMES DIVIDE MODULUS function performs the same calculation as the TIMES DIVIDE function except that both the remainder and the quotient are stored. It is described symbolically as:

n1 n2 n3 */MOD—→remainder quotient

The quotient is placed on top of the stack and the remainder below it, as demonstrated in the following examples:

      5 3 2 */MOD . . 7 1 OK

-7 5 4 */MOD . . -8 -3   OK

Again, the times divide modulus function is more accurate than the sequence {n1 n2 * n3 /MOD} because of the double precision intermediate product.
    The SIGN function applies the arithmetic sign of the value on the top of the stack to the value below it. This function is described symbolically as:

n1 n2 +- ⟶ n3

where n3=sign(n2)*n1. The values n1 and n2 are removed from the stack and the result is placed in the stack, as demonstrated in the following examples:

4 -5 +- . -4   OK

-4 -5 +- . 4   OK

-4 5 +- . -4   OK

-4 5 +- . . -4 0   EMPTY STACK

The mathematical functions in FORTH represent a basic set that can be expanded by the user through the definitional facility. When a function is defined in FORTH, it is used in exactly the same manner that built-in functions are used.

COMPLEMENT ARITHMETIC

    During internal computer operations, FORTH recognizes 16-bit or 32-bit numbers stored in binary two's complement notation. What this means is that a positive integer is stored in true form and a negative integer is stored in two's complement form. This section covers 16-bit operations; 32-bit operations are covered in the chapter on double-precision arithmetic.

In a computer, integer values can be stored in either "signed magnitude" representation or "two's complement" form. In SIGNED MAGNITUDE REPRESENTATION, a numeric value is expressed in true form to which is prefixed a sign digit, as in the following skeleton:

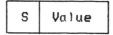

S refers to the sign and Value is the computer representtion of the number. Normally, the digits 0 for + and 1 for - are used as signs so the signed-magnitude representations of +5 and -5 are:

Representation of +5: 0000000000000101

Representation of -5: 1000000000000101

When numbers are stored in signed-magnitude representation, the methods used for internal computer operations must take the sign into consideration. FORTH does not use signed-magnitude representation!

With TWO'S COMPLEMENT arithmetic, negative numbers are stored in two's complement form and the internal logic of the microprocessor is simplified by taking this fact into account.

The BASE COMPLEMENT of a number N is defined as:

$$\text{Complement of } N = b^n - N$$

where "b" is the base and "n" is the number of digits in N. More specifically, $b^n - 1$ is the largest number that can be represented with n digits. Thus, the ten's complement of 435 is 565 and the two's complement of 1010 is 0110. In the computer, numbers are stored in fixed-length memory locations or arithmetic registers, so the number of digits in a number is fixed. In the binary number system, the two's complement of a number can be developed by inspection. All zeros are converted to ones, all ones are converted to zeros, and 1 is added to the resulting value. For example, the two's complement of the binary number 101 is computed as follows:

```
0000000000000101   (original value)
1111111111111010   (convert 1 to 0 and 0 to 1)
             +1    (add 1)
1111111111111011   (two's complement)
```

The primary advantages of using complement arithmetic are: (1) It is relatively simple to develop the two's complement; and (2) Arithmetic operations are executed without regard to the size.
    Typical addition operations using complement arithmetic are:

```
 0000000000000110   (6)     0000000000000110    (6)
+0000000000001101  +(13)   +1111111111110011  +(-13)
 0000000000010011   (19)    1111111111111001    (-7)


 1111111111111010   (-6)    1111111111111010    (-6)
+0000000000001101  +(13)   +1111111111110011  +(-13)
1 0000000000000111   (7)   1 1111111111101101   (-19)
↑                          ↑
Carry is discarded         Carry is discarded
```

Subtraction has similar advantages and is performed by taking the two's complement of the subtrahend and adding it to the minuend, as demonstrated in the following examples:

```
0000000000001101  (13)   0000000000000110     (6)
-0000000000000110 -(6)  -0000000000001101    -(13)
 0000000000001101  (13)   0000000000000110      (6)
+1111111111111010 +(-6) +1111111111110011    +(-13)
1 0000000000000111  (7)   1111111111111001     (-7)
↑
Carry is discarded
```

```
 0000000000000110     (6)   1111111111110011  (-13)
-1111111111110011   -(-13) -1111111111111010  -(-6)
 0000000000000110     (6)   1111111111110011  (-13)
+0000000000001101  +(13)  +0000000000000110   +(6)
 0000000000010011    (19)   1111111111111001   (-7)
```

To sum up, two's complement arithmetic provides the
benefits of other methods of representation, while
at the same time simplifying internal computer
operations. The leftmost bit can also be regarded
as a sign bit, since a negative value always begins
with a one bit and a positive value always begins
with a zero bit.

The MINUS operation in FORTH changes the sign
of the value on the top of th stack and is
described symbolically as:

                n1 MINUS ──→ -n2

where "n1" is the value on the top of the stack.
When the word {MINUS} is encountered by FORTH, it
removes the top value from the stack, takes its
two's complement, and places the result in the
stack. Figure 4.2 demonstrates the MINUS
operation, as well as other aspects of complement
arithmetic.

In some versions of FORTH, the word NEGATE is
used in place of MINUS. This is simply the process
of evolution, wherein specificity is incorporated
into the language definitions.

Many computers incorporate facilities for
complement arithmetic and for storing negative
numbers in two's complement notation. That is the

primary reason that this section of the chapter
exists.   Other computers do not utilize complement
arithmetic.   The meaning of a FORTH program is not
necessarily dependent upon a particular type of
hardware, except when "bit level" programming is
involved.   However, it is useful to note that the
FORTH   concept   embodies   two's   complement
representation.

```
-3 MINUS . 3  OK
175 MINUS . -175  OK
5 BINARY . 101  OK
DECIMAL -5 BINARY . -101  OK
111111111111111 DECIMAL . -32767  OK
BINARY  OK
1000000000000000 DECIMAL . -32768  OK
BINARY  OK
1111111111111111 . -1  OK
1111111111111111 DECIMAL . -1  OK
BINARY  OK
111111111111111 1 + . -1000000000000000  OK
```

Figure 4.2
Examples of complement arithmetic.

VOCABULARY

A familiarity with the following terms and FORTH words is necessary for learning the FORTH language:

    +
    -
    *
    /
    +-
    */
    ABS
    Complement arithmetic
    DEPTH
    DROP
    DUP
    -DUP
    ?DUP
    MAX
    MIN
    MINUS
    MOD
    /MOD
    */MOD
    NEGATE
    Number base
    OVER
    PICK
    ROLL
    ROT
    Signed magnitude representation
    SWAP
    Two's complement
    Word

EXERCISES

1. Write FORTH statements to perform the following calculations:

  a. Evaluate ax+b, for a=2, b=3, and x=5.

  b. Evaluate 2(n+1)(n+1) for n=4.

  c. Evaluate n(n+1)(n+2) for n=5.

  d. Evaluate ax/b for a=4, b=2, and x=5.

  e. Evaluate aa+bb for a=3 and b=4.

2. Give the result from performing the following
operations:

```
-4 13 +
6 -5 -
-9 -3 *
-11 2 /
17 -8 MOD
-19 4 /MOD
2 1 DUP
9 3 7 SWAP
16 3 -8 DROP
9 3 7 OVER
-1 6 3 -8 ROT
-1 6 3 -8 2 ROLL
6 -2 -DUP
4 -1 ABS
-13 -63 MAX
14 -6 MIN
7 4 3 */
-11 3 2 */MOD
63 -37 +-
```

3. Give the results from executing the following
FORTH statements:

  a. 16 MINUS 5 + 2 MOD .
  b. 6 3 DUP ROT 4 */MOD DROP + .
  c. 23 3 /MOD SWAP / DUP * .
  d. 15 4 MINUS 11 */MOD * 2 + .
  e. 47 13 MINUS /MOD MAX ABS DUP + .

Chapter 5.   CONSTANTS, VARIABLES, AND MEMORY
             OPERATIONS

A FORTH program is developed as a set of
"function" calls. New words are defined from old
words (i.e., words already defined) until a single
definition represents the whole program. Since it
is relatively easy to split a function into
subfunctions, there is a lesser need in FORTH to
utilize named variables than in conventional
programming languages. The stack is normally used
for temporary storage. When the number of entries
in the stack is too many to keep track of, then a
function is usually subdivided. There are times,
however, when named variables are necessary for a
particular application or for implicit commenting
available through meaningful variable names. The
FORTH language includes facilities for defining
constants and variables and for executing "store"
and "fetch" operations.

CONSTANTS

A CONSTANT is a value that does not change
during the execution of a program. If the same
value is used several places in a program, it saves
memory space to define it as a constant. Another
advantage of using a constant is that its value is
specified in only one place in a program. If a
change to the constant were necessary, it would
only have to be changed once. If a constant
definition were not used, then values would be
scattered throughout the program. If a change were
then necessary, the programmer would have to search
out each value. Invariably, one or two occurrences
are missed resulting in less software reliability.
A constant is defined in FORTH with a statement
of the form:

value CONSTANT name

where "value" is the value of the constant and
"name" is the name by which it is referenced. The
following examples demonstrate the definition and

use of a constant:

6 CONSTANT SIX   OK

SIX . 6 OK

SIX 2 * . 12 OK

The word CONSTANT is an executable operation in
FORTH in comparison to nonexecutable declarations
in some programming languages. When the word
CONSTANT is encountered by FORTH, the value on the
top of the stack is used as the constant's value.
The word following CONSTANT is the name of the
constant. The value on the top of the stack is
removed.

   A constant is referenced by using its name, as
demonstrated in the preceding example. When the
name of a constant is encountered by FORTH, the
value of the constant is pushed into the stack.
Figure 5.1 gives several examples of the definition
and use of constants.

```
80 CONSTANT LINESIZE   OK
60 CONSTANT PAGESIZE   OK
LINESIZE PAGESIZE * . 4800  OK
LINESIZE PAGESIZE * CONSTANT BUFSIZE   OK
BUFSIZE . 4800  OK
```

Figure 5.1
Definition and use of FORTH constants.

VARIABLES

   A VARIABLE is a quantity that can change during
the execution of a program. When a variable is
defined, its location is established and its
initial value is specified. A variable's location,
specified as a memory address, does not change.

The value of a variable is changed when a store operation is made to its memory address.
    A variable is defined in FORTH with a statement of the form:

                value VARIABLE name

where "value" is the initial value of the variable and "name" is the name by which it is referenced. The following examples demonstrate the definition of a variable:

        16 VARIABLE PCL   OK

        10 VARIABLE DX   OK

        -173 VARIABLE RIMIT   OK

The word VARIABLE is an executable operation in FORTH that uses the value on the top of the stack as the initial value of the variable. When the word VARIABLE is encountered by FORTH, the value on the top of the stack is removed as the initial value of the variable and the word following VARIABLE is the name of the variable.
    Each time the word VARIABLE is encountered by FORTH, a new variable is defined. Therefore, the word should not be used to change the value of a variable. VARIABLE should only be used to declare a variable initially.
    When the name of a variable is encountered by FORTH, the address of the variable is placed on the stack. The address is used with store and fetch operations.

                FETCH OPERATION

    The FETCH operation uses the value on the top of the stack as an address and is described symboliclly as:

$$addr \; @ \longrightarrow n$$

where "addr" is a memory address and "n" is the value stored at the specified address. The following examples demonstrate the fetch operation:

5 VARIABLE A   OK

A @ . 5   OK

25 CONSTANT TX   OK

TX A @ + . 30   OK

When the word {@} is encountered by FORTH, it removes the value on the top of the stack interpreting the value as an address. The contents of the specified address location are "fetched" from memory and pushed into the stack.

The fetch operation can be used to examine the contents of any location in memory, and is not limited exclusively to variables. In fact, absolute memory locations can be specified with the fetch operation giving the user complete access to the contents of ROM and RAM. For example, if the user wished to display the contents of binary location 1011011, the following statements would do the job:

BINARY   OK

1011011 @ . -100011111000   OK

The fetch operation should not be used with a constant because a reference to the name of a constant yields the value of the constant and not its memory address. The only case wherein a fetch operation to the value of a constant would be meaningful is when the constant value represents a memory address.

STORE OPERATION

The STORE operation is used to place a value in memory at a specified address and is described symbolically as:

n addr !

where "n" is the value to be placed in memory and "addr" is the memory address where the value should be placed. The address is on the top of the stack and the value is directly below it. When the word {!} is encountered by FORTH, the two top values are removed from the stack and the store operation is performed. The following statements demonstrate the "store" operation:

3 VARIABLE TEMP   OK

25 TEMP !   OK

TEMP @ . 25   OK

When a store operation to a memory location is performed, the previous contents of that location are lost.
    As with the fetch operation, the use of the store operation is not limited exclusively to variables. The contents of any memory location in RAM can be changed with the store operation. For example, if the user wished to place a 1 in hexadecimal location A3FE, the following statements would do the job:

HEX   OK

1 A3FE !   OK

A3FE @ . 1   OK

As with the fetch operation, the store operation should not be used with a constant because a reference to the name of a constant yields the

value of the constant and not its memory address.
The only case wherein a store operation to the
value of a constant would be meaningful is when the
constant value represents a memory address.

Figure 5.2 gives several examples of the
definition and use of variables and the fetch and
store operations.

```
8 VARIABLE A   OK
45 VARIABLE B   OK
A @ B @ SWAP B ! A !   OK
A @ . 45   OK
B @ . 8   OK
```

Figure 5.2
A set of FORTH operations that exchange
the values of variables A and B.

ADD TO MEMORY

The ADD TO MEMORY operatiion can be used to add
a value to the contents of a memory location.
While this operation can be programmed as a series
of FORTH operations, it occurs frequently enough to
warrant a special built-in function, which is
described symbolically as:

$$n \text{ addr} +!$$

where "n" is the value to be added to the contents
of the specified memory address and "addr" is the
memory address. The address is on the top of the
stack and the value is directly below it. When the
word {+!} is encountered by FORTH, the two top
values are removed from the stack. The contents of
the specified address are fetched from memory, the
given value is added to it, and the result is
stored in the memory location indicated by the
address. The following example demonstrates the
"add to memory" operation:

        3 VARIABLE BETA   OK

        2 BETA +!   OK

        BETA @ . 5   OK

The "add to memory" operation is representative of
a class of operations that a user can define to
extend FORTH to a particular application
environment.

                    THE DICTIONARY

     The heart of the FORTH system is a dictionary
that contains all FORTH words and their
definitions.   Whenever an entity is defined by the
user, it is placed in the dictionary.   The
dictionary entries that have been covered thusfar
are:

          o FORTH words
          o Colon definition names
          o Constant names
          o Variable names

     A dictionary entry name can consist of up to
any 31 keyboard characters, excluding the space
character.   The VLIST command can be used to list
the contents of the dictionary and Figure 5.3 gives
a sample listing.
     The complete listing of the dictionary is
lengthy and it is cumbersome to search through it
to determine if a particular entry is in the table
or not.   The "tick" comand, described symbolically
as:

                    word ⟶ addr

where "word" is the name of the entry and "addr" is
its address in the dictionary, can be used to find
out if the specified word is in the dictionary. If

```
VLIST
TASK    SEARCH   SRCH    ST    SW
COUNT-CHRS    EFL    #CHRS    SLINE
SCAN    EDIT    EDITOR    MON    DEMO
   LS    VLINE    HLINE    SCRN    PLOT
COLOR    TEXT    GR    CLEAR    (TXT)
(GR)    L    SCOPY    BSTR    SBTR
CODE    ASSEMBLER    RAND    URAND
RSEED    BUFFERS    BACKUP    DUMP
.ROW    .ASCII    .VALUES    .ADDRESS
SAVETURNKEY    INITIALIZEDISK
SAVESYSTEM    &SIZE    &DUMP-FORTH
&DUMP-RWTS    &DISK-DUMP    &RWTS-FMT
SECTORS    GET    LOAD    LK    JOIN
VLIST    INDEX    LIST    VHTAB
Y/NQUERY    WHERE    IND    PR    ?CARD
D=    DO=    D?    DMAX    DMIN    D>
D<    D-    2ROT    2SWAP    2DUP
2OVER    2DROP    -->    ?    .    .R
U.    U.R    D.    D.R    #S    #    SIGN
#>    <#    SPACES    &R/WSECT    FORGET
'    WHILE    ELSE    IF    REPEAT
AGAIN    END    UNTIL    +LOOP    LOOP
DO    THEN    ENDIF    BEGIN    BACK
MYSELF    REBOOT    ((COMPILE))
[COMPILE]    &R/W    &I/O    &DRV
DRIVE2    DRIVE1    ERRMSG    CALL
&RWTS    LOAD    MESSAGE    .LINE
(LINE)    BLOCK    EMPTY-BUFFERS
FLUSH    BUFFER    DRO    UPDATE    +BUF
M/MOD    */    */MOD    MOD    /    /MOD
*    M/    M*    MAX    MIN    DABS    ABS
D+-    +-    S->D    COLD    COLD1
HOME    ABORT    QUIT    (
DEFINITIONS    FORTH    VOCABULARY
IMMEDIATE    INTERPRET    ?STACK
DLITERAL    LITERAL    CREATE    ID.
ERROR    (ABORT)    -FIND    NUMBER
(NUMBER)    WORD    PAD    HOLD
BLANKS    ERASE    QUERY    EXPECT
."    (.")    -TRAILING    TYPE    COUNT
```

```
DOES>    <BUILDS   ;CODE    (;CODE)
DECIMAL   HEX    SMUDGE    ]    [
COMPILE   ?LOADING   ?CSP   ?PAIRS
?EXEC   ?COMP   ?ERROR   !CSP   PFA
NFA    CFA    LFA    LATEST    TRAVERSE
U<    -DUP    SPACE    ROT    >    =    -
C,    ,    ALLOT    HERE    2+    1+
DISKMAX    SLOT    HLD    R#    CSP
FLD    DPL    BASE    STATE    CURRENT
CONTEXT    OFFSET    SCR    OUT    IN
BLK    C/L    PREV    USE    LIMIT
FIRST    VOC-LINK    DP    FENCE
WARNING    WIDTH    TIB    CV    CH
+ORIGIN    B/SCR    B/BUF    BL    3    2
1    0    USER    2CONSTANT    2VARIABLE
2!    2@    VARIABLE    CONSTANT    EMIT
;    :    BCALC    -TEXT    ROLL    PICK
C!    !    C@    @    TOGGLE    +!    DUP
SWAP    DROP    OVER    DMINUS    MINUS
D+    +    <    0<    0=    R    R>    >R
LEAVE    ;S    RP!    SP!    SP@    XOR
OR    AND    U/    U*    FILL    CMOVE
KEYESC[    CR    ?TERMINAL    KEY
(EMIT)    ENCLOSE    (FIND)    DIGIT
I    (DO)    (+LOOP)    (LOOP)
0BRANCH    BRANCH    EXECUTE    CLIT
LIT
 OK
```

Figure 5.3
**A sample listing of the dictionary generated with
the VLIST command.**

the word is in the dictionary, then FORTH places
its address on the stack. If the word is not in
the dictionary, then FORTH responds with the word
followed by a question mark. Figure 5.4 contains
an example of the tick command.

As with all FORTH words, the "tick" symbol must
always be followed by a space.

The FORGET command can be used to delete an
entry from the dictionary; it is written as
follows:

FORGET word

where "word" is the name of the entry to be
deleted. Figure 5.4 additionally includes examples
of the FORGET command.

Caution should be taken when using the FORGET
command because it deletes the specified entry and
all entries defined after it was defined.

```
    SQR . SQR   ?
  : SQR DUP * ;   OK
  3 SQR . 9  OK
  '   SQR . 15692  OK
  6 VARIABLE A   OK
  21 VARIABLE B   OK
  ' A . 15704   OK
  ' B . 15712   OK
  FORGET B   OK
  ' B . B   ?
  FORGET SQR   OK
  ' SQR . SQR   ?
  ' A .   ?
```

Figure 5.4
Examples of the use of the tick
operation and FORGET command.

VOCABULARY

A general familiarity with the following terms and FORTH words is necessary for learning the FORTH language:

    +!
    CONSTANT
    Dictionary
    @ (fetch)
    FORGET
    ! (store)
    ' (tick)
    VARIABLE

EXERCISES

1. Define the following constants:

Name	Value
ONE	1
TWO	2
DX	15
DY	2*DX-1

2. Define the following variables:

Name	Value
X	321
Y	-6
W	X+Y-173

3. Write FORTH statements for the following statements using variables:

    A=A-1
    Y=A*X**2-B*X+C

where ** denotes exponentiation.

Chapter 6. DEFINITIONS AND TERMINAL
            OPERATIONS

Programming in FORTH is essentially the process
of extending the language. Every time a new
operation is defined in FORTH, the definition is
placed in the dictionary and becomes part of the
language. Through this process, a programmer can
build up a sophisticated set of operations that
pertain to a particular application environment.
This chapter covers colon definitions, which are an
essential part of FORTH programming, and terminal
input/output operations.

COLON DEFINITIONS

A colon definition is used to define an
operation in FORTH and consists of the following
elements:

- The initial colon (:)
- The name of the operation
- The body of the definition
- The terminal semicolon (;)

The initial colon, the name of the operation, and
the terminal semicolon are mandatory. The body of
the definition is optional; if present, however, it
must contain elements in the FORTH dictionary,
numerical values, or character literals.
    The structure of a colon definition is:

```
: name
  body of definition
;
```

wherein the textual structure is intended only to
improve readability, since FORTH is a free form
language. The following definition illustrates the
preceding concepts:

```
: INITIALIZE
  1 CONSTANT ONE
```

```
        2 CONSTANT TWO
        10 VARIABLE DX
        1000 VARIABLE LIMIT
      ;  OK
```

When a colon definition is entered into the FORTH system, it is placed in the dictionary for subsequent use in a FORTH statement. The initial colon and terminal semicolon must always be preceded and followed by at least one space character.

A colon definition is not executed until its name is present in a FORTH statement that causes the body of the definition to be invoked. Figure 6.1 gives examples of colon definitions and their invocation.

COMMENT LINES

A comment line can be entered at the keyboard in the execution or the definition mode by enclosing the comment line in parentheses, as follows:

(THIS IS A COMMENT LINE)

The initial left parenthesis must be followed by a space character. The right parenthesis ends the comment.

If a comment line is entered in the execution mode, FORTH responds immediately with the word OK. In this mode, a comment line can be used to annotate a listing of the display screen.

In the definition mode, a comment line is stored with the definition in which it is enclosed. When the defined operation is executed by FORTH, the comment line is ignored. However, the comment line serves to inform the reader of the meaning of the definition when it is listed. Figure 6.2 gives an example of comment lines in a function that exchanges the values of two variables.

```
0 VARIABLE X   OK
0 VARIABLE Y   OK
0 VARIABLE Z   OK
: LOAD-XYZ
  Z !
  Y !
  X !
;   OK
: LIST-XYZ
  X @ .
  Y @ .
  Z @ .
;   OK
10 20 30 LOAD-XYZ   OK
LIST-XYZ 10 20 30   OK
```

Figure 6.1
Colon definitions and their invocation.

```
: EXCHANGE  ( VALUES OF A AND B)
  ( STACK CONTENTS: A B)
  DUP        ( A B B)
  @          ( A B VB)
  ROT        ( B VB A)
  DUP        ( B VB A A)
  @          ( B VB A VA)
  4 ROLL     ( VB A VA B)
  !          ( VB A - A STORED)
  !          ( B STORED)
;   OK
24 VARIABLE TIME   OK
6 VARIABLE MONEY   OK
TIME MONEY EXCHANGE   OK
TIME @ . 6   OK
MONEY @ . 24   OK
```

Figure 6.2
Colon definition that exchanges the values of two variables and
demonstrates the use of comment lines.

DOT OPERATION

The DOT OPERATION outputs a number, followed by a space, to the printer or display. The dot operation uses the period (i.e., {.}) as a FORTH word and is described symbolically as:

n .

where "n" is the value to be displayed. The value is always placed on the output medium with a trailing space character. When the word {.} is encountered by FORTH, the top value is removed from the stack and the output operation is performed. The following example demonstrates the "dot" operation:

-13 173 DUP . . . 173 173 -13   OK

The dot operation is limited exclusively to the output of numerical values.

The dot operation displays a negative number in true form with a preceding minus sign. Positive values are displayed without a preceding plus sign.

The number to be displayed is converted from binary to an external form using the number base stored as a variable named BASE. A value can be entered in one number system whereby it is stored internally in binary. Output conversion can be made according to another base as follows:

DECIMAL OK
138 HEX . 8A OK
8A DECIMAL . 138   OK

The number displayed with the dot operation can be entered into the stack directly or result from a previous computation. the dot operation always outputs the value on the top of the stack.

DOT-R OPERATION

The DOT-R OPERATION displays a value while permitting the programmer to specify a field width. The dot-r operation uses the FORTH word {.R} as an operator symbol and is described symbolically as:

                    n width .R

where "n" is the value to be displayed and "width" is the field width. Both values are in the stack. The field width is on top and the value to be displayed is directly below it. When the word {.R} is encountered by FORTH, both values are removed from the stack and the output operation is performed. The output value is always right justified in the field, as follows:

```
( THIS LINE IS FOR ALIGNMENT )  OK
-13 6 173 8 .R .R        173    -13  OK
12345 2 .R 12345  OK
-125 3 .R -125  OK
```

If the number of characters in the number is less than the field width, then it is padded on the left with spaces. If the number of characters in the number including the algebraic sign, is greater than the field width, then the field width is extended as demonstrated above.

The dot-r operation adheres to the same output conversion rules as the dot operation. Numbers are always stored internally in binary and converted for output according to the existing number base.

CARRIAGE RETURN

During a terminal output operation, FORTH fills the output line until it is full, and then continues on the next line. If it is desired to resume the display on the next line, the programmer should insert a CARRIAGE RETURN into the FORTH statement or colon definition. The carriage return

is represented by the FORTH word {CR}, which must
be preceded and followed by a space character.
Figure 6.3 gives some examples of the use of the
carriage return.

CHARACTER LITERALS

A CHARACTER LITERAL may be displayed by
enclosing it in the FORTH words {."} and {"} as
follows:

." THIS IS A CHARACTER LITERAL"

where the word {."} must be followed by a space
character. The terminal word {"} ends the literal.
If a character literal is entered in the
execution mode, FORTH responds immediately by
displaying the literal without the enclosing FORTH
words. In the definition mode, the character
literal is saved as part of the colon definition.
When the defined function is subsequently executed,
the literal is displayed without the enclosing
FORTH words when it is encountered by FORTH.
Figure 6.4 contains examples of character literals.
FORTH words placed between the quotation marks
in a character literal are not interpreted as FORTH
words, but rather as keyboard characters to be
routinely displayed.

SCREEN OPERATIONS

Some versions of FORTH include a vertical and
horizontal tabbing feature that allows the cursor
to be moved to a specified position on the screen.
Once the cursor has been moved to the desired
position, the next input or output operation
proceeds from that point. The tabbing feature uses
the FORTH word {VHTAB}, described as follows:

n1 n2 VHTAB

```
-13 173 , CR , 173
-13  OK
: CUBE              ( OF N ON THE STACK)
   DUP              ( PREPARE TO PRINT N)
   CR 3 ,R          ( PRINT N)
   DUP DUP * *      ( COMPUTE CUBE)
   6 ,R             ( PRINT CUBE)
;  OK
12 CUBE
 12 1728  OK
25 CUBE
 25 15625  OK
```

Figure 6.3
The carriage return {CR} is used to begin output on a new line.

```
." THIS IS A TEST" THIS IS A TEST  OK
0 VARIABLE PAGECOUNT  OK
: PAGENUMBER
   PAGECOUNT DUP ( ADDR OF PAGE COUNT)
   @ 1 +            ( ADD 1 TO COUNT)
   DUP CR           ( DUP COUNT, START LINE)
   ." PAGE"         ( CHARACTER LITERAL)
   3 ,R             ( PRINT COUNT)
   SWAP !           ( STORE COUNT)
;  OK
PAGENUMBER
PAGE 1  OK
PAGENUMBER
PAGE 2  OK
```

Figure 6.4
Use of a character literal in the execution and definition modes.

where "n1" is the vertical screen position and "n2" is the horizontal screen position. When VHTAB is encountered by FORTH, "n1" and "n2" are removed from the stack, where "n1" is on the top of the stack and "n2" is directly below it. The cursor is then moved to the specified position.

   Another feature included in some versions of FORTH is the HOME command that clears the screen and moves the cursor to the upper left hand corner. Figure 6.5 lists a colon definition that includes the HOME and VHTAB operations.

```
: TITLE
  HOME
  10 20 VHTAB
  ." CHAPTER 7. CONTROL STRUCTURES"
; OK
```

Figure 6.5
Examples of the HOME and VHTAB operations.

SPACE CHARACTERS

   A space character can be inserted into the output line by using the FORTH words {SPACE} or {SPACES}. The FORTH word {SPACE} inserts a single space at the current line position. The word {SPACES} uses one value, described as follows:

n SPACES

where "n" is the number of spaces to be placed in the output line. For example, the following statement:

5 SPACES

would insert 5 spaces in the output line.

UNSIGNED OUTPUT

An unsigned number is one in which all of the bits in a word are interpreted as data bits. In a single-precision value, all sixteen bits represent data without an algebraic sign. In a doubl precision value all thirty-two bits represent data without an algebraic sign. This section covers unsigned output of single precision values.

Two operations are included in FORTH that give the programmer the capability of displaying unsigned numbers: the "u-dot" operation and the "u-dot-r" operation. The U-DOT OPERATION is similar to the dot operation except that all bits in the single precision value are treated as unsigned data bits. Thus all unsigned data values are effectively positive. The u-dot operation uses the FORTH word {U.} and is described symbolically as:

n U.

where "n" is the value to be displayed. As with the dot operation, the value is always placed on the output medium with a trailing space character. When the word {U.} is encountered by FORTH, the top value is removed from the stack and the output operation is performed. The following example demonstrates the u-dot operation:

-13 173 U. U. 173 65523 OK

The u-dot operation is limited exclusively to the output of numerical values.

The U-DOT-R operation is similar to the u-dot operation with the exception that it permits field width to be specified. The u-dot-r operations uses the FORTH word {U.R} and is described symbolically as:

n width U.R

where "n" is the value to be displayed and "width"
is the field width. Both values are in the stack.
The field width is on top and the value to be
displayed is directly below it.   When the word
{U.R} is encountered by FORTH, both values are
removed from the stack and the output operation is
performed.   The output value is always right
justified in the field, as follows:

(THIS LINE IS FOR ALIGNMENT) OK
-13 6 173 8 U.R U.R   173 65523 OK

    The same conversion rules that apply to signed
output also apply to unsigned output. The number
to be displayed is converted from internal binary
to the existing number base and then translated to
character form for output.
    If the number of characters in a number exceed
the field width specified with the u-dot-r
operation, then the field width is extended to
accomodate the actual value.

DISPLAY CONTENTS OF ADDRESS

    One of the most common sequences of FORTH
operations is {addr @ .}, which is used to display
the contents of an address. This basic operation
occurs frequently enough in FORTH programming to
warrant a symbol of its own, described as follows:

addr ?

where "addr" is the address of the location whose
contents should be displayed.   When FORTH
encounters the word {?}, the top entry is removed
from the stack. This is the address. The contents
of the indicated address are fetched from memory
and displayed in the form of a dot operation, as

indicated in the following example:

    <u>3 VARIABLE DELTA</u> OK

    <u>DELTA ? 3</u> OK

The "display contents of address" operation does not alter the contents of the stack after the specified address is removed.

VOCABULARY

A general familiarity with the following terms and FORTH words is necessary for learning the FORTH language:

```
:
;
(
)
.
"
."
?
.R
Carriage return
Character literal
Colon definition
Comment line
CR
HOME
SPACE
SPACES
U.
U.R
VHTAB
```

EXERCISES

1. Write a colon definition to raise a number to the fifth power.

2. Write a colon definition to print a title and
page number across the top of the screen.

3. Write a colon definition to add one to the value
of a variable in memory.

Chapter 7. CONTROL STRUCTURES

Logical Values

Comparison Operations

Logical Operations

DO Loop

IF Statement

EXIT and LEAVE Operations

Indefinite Loops

Vocabulary

Exercises

The control structures in FORTH provide the
capability for program looping and conditional
operations. Program looping facilities include the
DO loop, the UNTIL loop, and the WHILE loop. The
conditional operation in FORTH is the IF statement.
Several of the control structures use logical
values, comparison operations, and logical
operations, which are covered initially.

LOGICAL VALUES

A number has a logical value of "true" if its
value is nonzero and has a logical value of "false"
if its value is zero. Accordingly, a binary value
of 1 represents true and a binary value of 0
represents false. A logical value can be placed in
the stack directly or result from an arithmetic,
comparison, or logical operation.
A logical value is referred to as a "flag" in
FORTH terminology.

COMPARISON OPERATIONS

The comparison operations in FORTH and their
respective operator symbols, recognized as FORTH
words are:

OPERATION	FORTH WORD
Less than	<
Greater than	>
Equal to	=
Unsigned less than	U<
Less than zero	0<
Greater than zero	0>
Equal to zero	0=

These operations are defined on 16-bit integer
values. Double precision operations are covered in
a separate chapter.

The LESS THAN operation in FORTH is described symbolically as:

$$n1 \; n2 \; < \longrightarrow flag$$

where "n1" is the leftmost operand and "n2" is the rightmost operand in the mathematical expression n1<n2. The operands are entered in the same order as they would be entered in ordinary mathematical notation. When FORTH encounters the word {<}, the top two values are removed from the stack and the comparison operation (i.e., n1<n2) is performed. If the value of n1 is less than the value of n2, then a "true" value of 1 is pushed into the stack. Otherwise, a "false" value of 0 is pushed into the stack. The following examples demonstrate the less than operation:

2 3 < . 1   OK

173 -13 < . 0   OK

-43 6 < . 1   OK

The GREATER THAN operation in FORTH is described symbolically as:

$$n1 \; n2 \; > \longrightarrow flag$$

where "n1" is the leftmost operand and "n2" is the rightmost operand in the mathematical expression n1>n2. The operands are entered in the same order as they would be entered in ordinary mathematical notation. When FORTH encounters the word {>}, the top two values are removed from the stack and the comparison operation (i.e., n1>n2) is performed. If the value of n1 is greater than the value of n2, then a "true" value of 1 is pushed into the stack. Otherwise, a "false" value of 0 is pushed into the stack. The following examples demonstrate the greater than operation:

173 -13) . 1 OK
_____

2 48) . 0 OK
_____

-4 -59) . 1 OK
_____

    The EQUAL TO operation in FORTH is described
symbolically as:

                n1 n2 =——►flag

where "n1" is the leftmost operand and "n2" is the
rightmost operand in the mathematical expression
n1=n2.   The operands are entered in the same order
as they would be entered in ordinary mathematical
notation.   When FORTH encounters the word {=}, the
top two values are removed from the stack and the
equal to operation (i.e., n1=n2) is performed.   If
the value of n1 is equal to the value of n2, then a
"true" value of 1 is pushed into the stack.
Otherwise, a "false" value of 0 is pushed into the
stack.   The following examples demonstrate the
equal to operation:

    54 54 = . 1 OK
_____

    23 -23 = . 0 OK
_____

    -31 -31 = . 1 OK
_____

    The UNSIGNED LESS THAN operation in FORTH is
described symbolically as:

                u1 u2 U<——►flag

where "u1" is the leftmost operand and "u2" is the
rightmost operand in the mathematical expression
u1<u2.   This operation is the same as {<} except
that the algebraic sign of the operands is ignored

and the full sixteen bits of the single precision
value are interpreted as data bits. The operands
are entered in the same order as they would be
entered in ordinary mathematical notation. When
FORTH encounters the word {U<}, the top two values
are removed from the stack and the comparison
operation (i.e., u1<u2) is performed. If the
absolute value of u1 is less than the value of u2,
then a "true" value of 1 is pushed into the stack.
Otherwise, a "false" value of 0 is pushed into the
stack. The following examples demonstrate the
unsigned less than operation:

2 3 U< . 1 OK

2 -3 U< . 1 OK

-3 -2 U< . 1 OK

The LESS THAN ZERO operation in FORTH is
described symbolically as:

n 0<———▶flag

where "n" is a value to be compared with zero, as
in the mathematical expression n<0. When FORTH
encounters the word {0<}, the top value is removed
from the stack and its value is compared with zero.
If the value of n is less than zero, then a "true"
value of 1 is pushed into the stack. Otherwise, a
"false" value of 0 is pushed into the stack. The
following examples demonstrate the "less than zero"
operation:

-13 0< . 1 OK

139 0< . 0 OK

The GREATER THAN ZERO operation in FORTH is

described symbolically as:

$$n\ 0) \longrightarrow flag$$

where "n" is a value to be compared with zero, as in the mathematical expression n>0. When FORTH encounters the word {0>}, the top value is removed from the stack and its value is compared with zero. If the value of n is greater than zero, then a "true" value of 1 is pushed into the stack. The following examples demonstrate the "greater than zero" operation:

<u>139 0> . 1 OK</u>

<u>-13 0> . 0 OK</u>

The EQUAL TO ZERO operation in FORTH is described symbolically as:

$$n\ 0= \longrightarrow flag$$

where "n" is a value to be compared with zero, as in the mathematical expression n=0. When FORTH encounters the word {0=}, the top value is removed from the stack and its value is compared with zero. If the value of n is equal to zero, then a "true" value of 1 is pushed into the stack. Otherwise, a "false" value of 0 is pushed into the stack. The following examples demonstrate the "equal to zero" operation:

<u>-13 0= . 0 OK</u>

<u>1 0= . 0 OK</u>

<u>0 0= . 1 OK</u>

The "equal to zero" operation performs the Boolean

NOT operation on binary values.

LOGICAL OPERATIONS

The logical operations in FORTH and their respective operator symbols, recognized as FORTH words are:

OPERATION	FORTH WORD
Logical and	AND
Logical or	OR
Logical exclusive or	XOR
Logical not	NOT

Logical operations in FORTH are applied in a bitwise fashion to 32-bit operands held in the stack. Each logical operation yields a 32-bit result which is placed in the stack.

The AND operation in FORTH is described symbolically as:

$$n1 \ n2 \ AND \longrightarrow n3$$

where "n1" and "n2" are the operands in the mathematical expression n1 n2 and "n3" is the logical result. When FORTH encounters the word {AND}, the top two values are removed from the stack and the "and" operation (i.e., n1 n2) is executed. The operation is performed on a bit-by-bit fashion according to the following table:

∧	0	1
0	0	0
1	0	1

The following examples demonstrate the "and" operation:

```
BINARY  OK

1 0 AND . 0  OK

1 1 AND . 1  OK

0 0 AND . 0  OK

101011001 100110011 AND . 100010001  OK
```

The   OR   operation   in   FORTH   is   described symbolically as:

$$n1 \ n2 \ OR \longrightarrow n3$$

where   "n1"   and   "n2"   are   the   operands   in   the mathematical   expression   n1vn2   and   "n3"   is   the logical   result.   When   FORTH   encounters the word {OR}, the top two values are removed from the stack and   the   "or"   operation   (i.e., n1vn2)   is   executed. The   operation   is   performed on a bit-by-bit fashion according to the following table:

```
v | 0  1
--+-----
0 | 0  1
1 | 1  1
```

The   following   examples   demonstrate   the   "or" operation:

```
BINARY  OK

1 0 OR . 1  OK

1 1 OR . 1  OK

0 0 OR . 0  OK

101011001 100110011 OR . 101111011  OK
```

The EXCLUSIVE OR operation in FORTH is described symbolically as:

$$n1\ n2\ XOR \longrightarrow n3$$

where "n1" and "n2" are the operands in the mathematical expression $\sim(n1=n2)$ and "n3" is the logical result. When FORTH encounters the word {XOR}, the top two values are removed from the stack and the "exclusive or" operation is executed. The operation is performed on a bit-by-bit fashion according to the following table:

$\neq$	0	1
0	0	1
1	1	0

The following examples demonstrate the "exclusive or" operation:

BINARY OK

1 0 XOR . 1 OK

0 0 XOR . 0 OK

1 1 XOR . 0 OK

101011001 100110011 XOR . 1101010 OK

The NOT operation in FORTH is described symbolically as:

$$n1\ NOT \longrightarrow n2$$

where "n1" is the operand and "n2" is the logical result. When FORTH encounters the word {NOT}, the top value is removed from the stack and the "not" operation is executed. The operation is performed on a bit-by-bit fashion according to the following table:

```
  ~ | 0  1
    |——————
    | 1  0
```

The following examples demonstrate the "not" operation:

    BINARY OK

    1 NOT U. 1111111111111110 OK

    0 NOT U. 1111111111111111 OK

    101011001 NOT U. 1111111010100110 OK

    The logical operations are conveniently used for masking operations, wherein it is desired to keep or eliminate specified bits in a field. The following example demonstrates a case where it is necessary to keep the low-order four bits of a binary field and make the other high-order bits zero:

    BINARY OK

    101011001 VARIABLE DATA OK

    DATA @ 1111 AND DATA ! OK

    DATA ? 1001 OK

Unlike the logical bit-by-bit operations, the control structures in FORTH inspect a stack item for a zero or non-zero condition when performing conditional operations.

DO LOOP

Many algorithms require that a sequence of steps be repeated a fixed number of times. An algorithm of this type is usually programmed in one of two ways: (1) The program steps are replicated the required number of times; and (2) the program is written so that the same program steps are executed repetitively. The second method is preferred for complex or lengthy programs.

A series of statements to be executed repetitively is termed a LOOP; the statements that comprise the loop are termed the BODY OF THE LOOP; and one pass through the loop is termed an ITERATION. The number of iterations is governed by three control values: the initial value, the limit value, and the increment value, and the process usually operates as follows:

1. A CONTROL VARIABLE is set to an initial value.

2. The body of the loop is executed.

3. The value of the control variable is increased by the increment value.

4. The value of the control variable is compared with the limit value. If the limit value is reached or is exceeded, then the first executable operation following the body of the loop is executed.

5. Execution of the loop continues with step 2.

In FORTH, a loop of this kind is called a DO LOOP. Figure 7.1 gives an example of a DO loop that prints the numbers 0 through 9. The components of the DO loop in Figure 7.1 are identified as follows:

```
    10 0            Limit value, initial value
  ┌──────────┐
  │ DO       │
  │   CR I . │      DO loop
  │ LOOP     │
  └──────────┘
```

where

    Limit value: 10
    Initial value: 0
    Body of loop: CR I .
    Increment value: set implicitly to 1

The control variable is maintained internally by
FORTH, and the FORTH word {I} places the value of
the control variable in the stack. The word {I} is
not an ordinary variable. It is a command to FORTH
to place the current value of the control variable
in the stack. The limit value should always be set
at one more than the intended limit by the
programmer.

```
: TOTEN
  10 0            ( CONTROL VALUES)
  DO              ( BEGINS LOOP)
    CR I .        ( BODY OF LOOP)
  LOOP            ( ENDS LOOP)
; OK
TOTEN
0
1
2
3
4
5
6
7
8
9  OK
```

Figure 7.1
A DO loop that prints the numbers 0 through 9.

It should be noted that one pass is always made
through the loop before the value of the control
variable is compared against the limit. Figure 7.2
gives a DO loop in which the initial value is
greater than the value but is still executed one
time.

```
: ONETIME
  5 10        ( LIMIT VALUE = 5)
  DO          ( INIT VALUE = 10)
    CR I .
  LOOP
; OK
ONETIME
10   OK
```

Figure 7.2
One pass is made through a DO loop even if the initial value
is greater than the limit value.

When the DO loop is executed, the value on the
top of the stack is taken as the initial control
value and the value directly below it in the stack
is taken as the limit value plus one. The
increment value is automatically set to one. The
operations between the FORTH words {DO} and {LOOP}
constitute the body of the loop that are executed
during each iteration. The DO loop executes by
increasing the value of the control variable by one
after each pass through the loop until the limit
value is reached or exceeded.

A Fibonacci series is a set of numbers of the
form:

        1 1 2 3 5 8 13 21 34 55 . . .

where the Ith number is the sum of the previous two
values. Figure 7.3 gives a colon definition
containing a DO loop that computes Fibonacci
numbers. In this case, the control variable is

used only as a counter since it is not referenced
in the body of the loop. Figure 7.4 gives a colon
definition, containing a DO loop, that computes N
factorial.   In this case, the control values are
not entered directly, but a minor computation is
performed to place the desired value, i.e., N+1, on
the stack.

```
: FIBONACCI
  1 DUP DUP DUP    ( SET UP INIT VALUES)
  CR . .           ( PRINT FIRST 2 VALUES)
  11 1             ( LOOP 10 TIMES)
  DO
     DUP ROT +     ( COMPUTE NEXT ELEMENT)
     DUP .         ( PRINT IT)
  LOOP
; OK
FIBONACCI
1 1 2 3 5 8 13 21 34 55 89 144  OK
```

Figure 7.3
A loop that generates Fibonacci numbers.

     A variation to the DO loop structure permits
the increment value to be established by the
programmer.   As an indication of how this facility
works, consider the DO loop in Figure 7.5 that
prints the even integers between 2 and 20
inclusive.   The structure is the same as the
conventional DO loop except that the FORTH word
{+LOOP} is used to close the loop and the value of
2 is pushed into the stack just prior to the word.
The {+LOOP} operation uses the value on the top of
the stack as the increment value.
     A "varying" increment can be used to make the
value of the control variable go backwards, as in
Figure 7.6 that generates a number and its square
as the index goes from 10 to zero. This program
demonstrates a case where the loop index is
referenced twice in the same loop. In each case,

```
: FACTORIAL    ( OF N)
  ." = "       ( DISPLAY EQUALS SIGN)
  1 +          ( LOOP N TIMES)
  1            ( RUNNING PRODUCT)
  SWAP 2       ( SET UP: 1 N+1 2)
  DO
    I *        ( COMPUTE FACTORIAL)
  LOOP
  .            ( DISPLAY RESULT)
; OK
5 FACTORIAL = 120  OK
7 FACTORIAL = 5040  OK
```

Figure 7.4
Do loop using a control variable to compute N factorial.

```
: 2LOOP
  21 2       ( LIMIT=20, INIT=2)
  DO
    CR I .   ( PRINT NUMBER)
  2          ( INCREMENT=2)
  +LOOP
; OK
2LOOP
2
4
6
8
10
12
14
16
18
20   OK
```

Figure 7.5
A DO loop illustrating an increment value of 2. Note that
+LOOP Is used to close the loop.

```
: RSQUARE
  0 10          ( LIMIT=1, INIT=10)
  DO
    CR I .      ( PRINT NUMBER)
    I DUP * . ( PRINT SQUARE)
-1
+LOOP
;  OK
RSQUARE
10 100
9 81
8 64
7 49
6 36
5 25
4 16
3 9
2 4
1 1  OK
```

Figure 7.6
A DO loop with an index running backwards.

it yields the same value, because it is an
operation that simply places the current index on
the stack.   This fact is further demonstrated in
Figure 7.7 that contains a nested loop.
    When loops are nested, it is sometimes
desirable to reference the index of the next outer
loop.   This operation can be performed through the
use of the word {J}.   When the word {J} is
encountered by FORTH, it pushes the current value
of the index of the next outer loop into the stack.
    When a loop index runs in the positive
direction, the limit value should be set at one
more than the intended limit. When a loop index
runs in the negative direction, the limit value
should be set at one less than the intended limit.

```
: NESTEDLOOP
  10 0
  DO                              ( **********)
    CR I . .                      (          *)
    0 3                           (          *)
    DO                            ( *****    *)
      CR 5 SPACES I .             (     *    *)
      -1                          (     *    *)
    +LOOP                         ( *****    *)
  2                               (          *)
  +LOOP                           ( **********)
; OK
NESTED LOOP
0
        3
        2
        1
2
        3
        2
        1
4
        3
        2
        1
6
        3
        2
        1
8
        3
        2
        1  OK
```

Figure 7.7
Nested loops demonstrating the use of the FORTH word {I}.

IF STATEMENT

The IF statement permits a series of FORTH operations to be executed on a conditional basis, as suggested by the following structure:

```
IF
  FORTH operations
ELSE
  FORTH operations
THEN
```

The IF statement tests the value on the top of the stack, removing it. If it is true (i.e., nonzero), the operations following the word {IF} up to the word {ELSE} are executed. Then, control passes to the statement following the word {THEN}. If the value on the top of the stack is false (i.e., zero), the operations following the word {ELSE} up to the word {THEN} are executed, and control passes to the statement following the word {THEN}. The following IF statement, for example, tests a number on the top of the stack and prints whether it is zero or nonzero:

```
IF
  ." NONZERO"
ELSE
  ." ZERO"
THEN
```

This statement is included in Figure 7.8 that depicts it in an operational setting.

The ELSE part of an IF statement is optional. If it is not present, then the "false" case simply drops through to the word THEN, where execution resumes. This option is demonstrated in the program in Figure 7.9, which tests the value on the top of the stack and changes its sign if it is negative.

```
: TESTIT
  IF
    CR ." NONZERO"
  ELSE
    CR ." ZERO"
  THEN
; OK
0 TESTIT
ZERO  OK
-1 TESTIT
NONZERO  OK
```

Figure 7.8
An example of the If-ELSE-THEN statement that displays
whether a number is nonzero or zero.

IF statements can be nested as suggested by the following skeleton:

```
IF      <------|
  A            |
  B            |
  IF    <---|  |
    C       |  |
    D       |  |
  ELSE      |  |
    E       |  |
    F       |  |
  THEN  <---|  |
ELSE            |
  G             |
  H             |
THEN    <------|
```

Statements can be organized in this fashion as long as one statement is wholly contained in another one; they may not overlap.

Figure 7.10 gives a program to "make changes"

that demonstrates the use of nested loops.

```
: MAKEPOS
  DUP          ( DUP VALUE FOR TESTING)
  0<           ( TEST IF NEGATIVE)
  IF
    MINUS      ( CHANGE SIGN)
  THEN
;  OK
5 MAKEPOS . 5  OK
-73 MAKEPOS . 73  OK
```

Figure 7.9
An example of the IF-THEN statement that makes the top
value on the stack positive.

EXIT AND LEAVE OPERATIONS

The MAKECHANGE program in Figure 7.10 includes
the EXIT operation that can be used to exit from a
colon definition. When the word {EXIT} is
encountered by FORTH, an exit is made from the
defined procedure in which it is included. The
exit operation may not be used from within a DO
loop.

The LEAVE operation forces an exit from a DO
loop by setting the index value equal to the limit
value. When the respective {LOOP} or {+LOOP} is
encountered by FORTH, a normal exit from the loop
is performed. Figure 7.11 contains a program that
computes the largest factor of a number; it
demonstrates the LEAVE operation.

INDEFINITE LOOPS

With many algorithms, the number of iterations
is not known beforehand and is discovered only
during the course of computation. A loop of this

```
: MAKECHANGE
  -DUP
  IF
    50 /MOD
    -DUP
    IF
      CR . ." HALVES"
    THEN
    -DUP
    IF
      25 /MOD
      -DUP
      IF
        CR . ." QUARTERS"
      THEN
      -DUP
      IF
        10 /MOD
        -DUP
        IF
          CR . ." DIMES"
        THEN
        -DUP
        IF
          5 /MOD
          -DUP
          IF
            CR . ." NICKELS"
          THEN
          -DUP
          IF
            CR . ." PENNIES"
          THEN
        THEN
      THEN
    THEN
  ELSE
    CR ." NO CHANGE"
  THEN
  CR ." *** THANK YOU ***"
;  OK
63 MAKECHANGE
```

```
1 HALVES
1 DIMES
3 PENNIES
*** THANK YOU ***   OK
```

Figure 7.10
A program to "make change" that demonstrates the
use of nested IF statements.

```
0 VARIABLE N   OK
0 VARIABLE NOTDONE   OK
: LGFACTOR        ( OF N)
  DUP DUP
  CR ." LARGEST FACTOR OF " . ." IS "
  N !
  1 NOTDONE !    ( SET NOT DONE FLAG)
  1              ( FINAL LOOP VALUE)
  SWAP 2 /       ( N/2 IS INIT VAL)
  DO
    N @ I MOD    ( N/I -> REM)
    0=
    IF
      I .        ( PRINT FACTOR)
      0 NOTDONE !
      LEAVE
    THEN
    -1
  +LOOP
  NOTDONE @
  IF
    1 .
  THEN
;  OK
51 LGFACTO
LARGEST FACTOR OF 51 IS 17   OK
```

Figure 7.11
A program that computes the largest factor of a number
and demonstrates the LEAVE operation.

Kind is Known as an INDEFINITE LOOP.
    FORTH includes two looping facilities to handle
indefinite loops, and these facilities correspond
to the "do while" and "do until" structures in
structured programming. Figure 7.12 depicts the do
while and do until structures. With the DO WHILE
loop, the test is performed beforehand, and the
block of code is executed only if the conditional
test yields a true value. With the DO UNTIL loop,
the test is performed afterwards, and continued
execution of the loop is performed only if the
conditional test yields a false value. In other
words, the loop is executed until a prespecified
condition is met. With the DO UNTIL loop, the
block of code is always executed at least once,
whereas with the DO WHILE loop, the block of code
may not be executed at all.

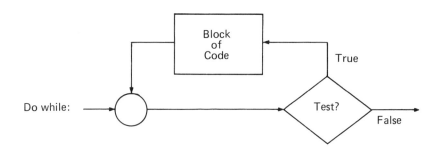

Do while:

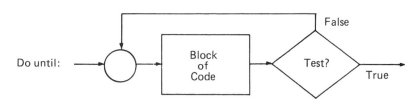

Do until:

Figure 7.12
The "do while" and "do until" structures in structured programming.

The BEGIN..WHILE..REPEAT statement structure in FORTH performs the do while loop and has the following structure:

```
BEGIN
  Operations for the conditional test
WHILE
  Operations for the loop
REPEAT
```

When FORTH encounters the BEGIN..WHILE..REPEAT structure, the operations between the FORTH words {BEGIN} and {WHILE} are executed. This is intended to be the conditional part of the loop. The FORTH word {WHILE} then tests the value on the top of the stack. If it is true (i.e., nonzero), then the operations between the FORTH words {WHILE} and {REPEAT} are executed. Upon encountering the word {REPEAT}, FORTH loops back to {BEGIN} and the process continues. If the value on the top of the stack is false when the word {WHILE} is encountered by FORTH, then FORTH continues execution with the operation following {REPEAT}. When using the BEGIN..WHILE..REPEAT structure, it is the programmer's responsibility to place the needed conditional operations between BEGIN and WHILE.

Figure 7.13 gives a simple program to illustrate the idea of a BEGIN..WHILE..REPEAT loop. The program prints a list of odd numbers and their squares. Statement numbered (1) sets the initial value for the loop counter. Statement numbered (2) begins the loop. Statement numbered (3) duplicates the loop counter for a conditional test and then performs a comparison operation with the limit of 20. Statement numbered (4) performs the WHILE test. If the result of the comparison is true, then execution continues with the operation after the FORTH word {WHILE}. If it is false, execution continues with the operation that follows the FORTH word {REPEAT}. Statement numbered (5) prints the loop counter and its squares. Statement numbered (6) adds an increment of 2 to the loop counter, which is on the top of the stack. Statement

numbered (7) passes control to the first operation
after the FORTH word {BEGIN}, and statement
numbered (8) removes the final loop value from the
stack.

```
: ODDSQUARES
  1                                ( 1 )
  BEGIN                            ( 2 )
    DUP 20 <                       ( 3 )
  WHILE  .                         ( 4 )
    CR DUP . DUP DUP * .           ( 5 )
    2 +                            ( 6 )
  REPEAT                           ( 7 )
  DROP                             ( 8 )
;  OK
ODDSQUARES
1 1
3 9
5 25
7 49
9 81
11 121
13 169
15 225
17 289
19 361   OK
```

Figure 7.13
A program that lists odd numbers and their squares to
demonstrate the BEGIN. .WHILE. .REPEAT loop.

A second form of the GREATEST COMMON DIVISOR
algorithm involves the modulus function. The
algorithm, which computes the greatest common
divisor of A and B, is listed as follows:

1. Enter A and B

2. If B is greater than A, exchange them

3. Divide A by B giving the remainder R.

4. Replace A by B (i.e., A   B)

5. Replace B by R (i.e., B   R)

6. If R)0, continue with step 3. Otherwise, A
is the greatest common divisor.

The actual calculations can be listed as follows:

GCD of 44 and 28			GCD of 10 and 8		
A	B	R	A	B	R
44	28	16	10	8	2
28	16	12	8	2	0
16	12	4	2	0	0
4	0	0	Result is 2		
Result is 4					

Figure 7.14 gives a program that computes the
greatest common divisor using this algorithm; it
demonstrates the BEGIN..WHILE..REPEAT loop.   It
should be emphasized that the WHILE operation tests
any value that is on the top of the stack. If it
is true (i.e., nonzero), then execution of the loop
continues.   Otherwise, as covered previously,
execution of the indefinite loop is terminated.
     The greatest common divisor program in Figure
7.14 demonstrates the use of a "subprogram" named
?EXCHANGE that verifies that variable A is greater
than   variable   B.   The   rest of the program
essentially duplicates the given algorithm.
     The BEGIN..UNTIL statement structure in FORTH
performs   the   do until structure and has the
following structure:

```
0 VARIABLE A   OK
0 VARIABLE B   OK
: ?EXCHANGE           ( A B)
  SWAP                ( B A)
  DUP                 ( B A A)
  ROT                 ( A A B)
  DUP                 ( A A B B)
  ROT                 ( A B B A)
  >                   ( A B F)
  IF
    SWAP              ( A > B)
  THEN
;  OK
: GCD1
  EXCHANGE            ( A > B)
  B ! A !
  BEGIN
    B @               ( TEST B)
  WHILE
    A @ B @
    MOD               ( A MOD B)
    B @ A !           ( A <- B)
    B !               ( B <- REM)
  REPEAT
  A @                 ( A IS RESULT)
  CR .                ( PRINT RESULT)
;  OK
38 57 GCD1
19  OK
```

Figure 7.14
A program to compute the greatest common divisor
demonstrating the BEGIN..WHILE..REPEAT loop.

```
BEGIN
    Operations for the loop
    Operations for the conditional test
UNTIL
```

When FORTH encounters the BEGIN..UNTIL structure, the operations between the FORTH words {BEGIN} and {UNTIL} are executed. This is intended to be both the operational and conditional parts of the loop. It should be noted that the loop is always executed at least once because the conditional test will be at the end of the loop. The FORTH word {UNTIL} then tests the value on the top of the stack. If it is true (i.e., nonzero), then the execution of the loop has been completed and FORTH continues execution with the operation following {UNTIL}. If the value on the top of the stack is false when the word {UNTIL} is encountered by FORTH, then FORTH continues execution with the operation following the initial BEGIN. Essentially, this is the looping facility available with the BEGIN..UNTIL looping structure. It is the programmer's responsibility to place the needed conditional operations between BEGIN and UNTIL and in the appropriate operational sequence.

Figure 7.15 gives a simple program to illustrate the idea of a BEGIN..UNTIL loop. The program prints a list of even numbers and their squares and cubes. The two subprograms named SQR and CUBE compute the square and cube operations, respectively, of the value on the top of the stack. Statement numbered (1) sets the initial value for the loop counter. Statement numbered (2) begins the loop. Statement numbered (3) returns the carriage (to the printer) so that each value begins on a new line. Statements numbered (4), (5), and (6) display the loop counter, its square, and its cube, respectively. Statement numbered (7) increases the value of the loop counter by 2 and statement numbered (8) compares its value against the limit of 20. Statement numbered (9) tests the condition. If its value is false, execution of the

```
: SQR
  DUP *
;  OK
: CUBE
  DUP DUP
  * *
;  OK
: EVENS
  2                    ( 1 )
  BEGIN                ( 2 )
    CR                 ( 3 )
    DUP .              ( 4 )
    DUP SQR .          ( 5 )
    DUP CUBE .         ( 6 )
    2 +                ( 7 )
    DUP 20 =           ( 8 )
  UNTIL                ( 9 )
  DROP                 ( 10)
;  OK
EVENS
2 4 8
4 16 64
6 36 216
8 64 512
10 100 1000
12 144 1728
14 196 2744
16 256 4096
18 324 5832   OK
```

Figure 7.15
A program that lists even numbers, their squares, and
their cubes to demonstrate the BEGIN. .UNTIL loop.

loop continues. Otherwise, control drops through the loop to the next operation. Statement numbered (10) removes the final loop value from the stack.

Figure 7.16 gives another program for the greatest common divisor algorithm presented earlier in the chapter; it demonstrates the BEGIN..UNTIL loop. The user should compare this program with the program named GCD1 in Figure 7.14 to obtain the subtle difference between the two types of indefinite loops.

```
: GCD2
    ?EXCHANGE      ( A > B)
    B ! A !
    BEGIN
      A @ B @      ( SET UP A AND B)
      MOD DUP      ( A MOD B)
      B @ A !      ( A <- B)
      B !          ( B <- REM)
      0=           ( TEST FOR ZERO)
    UNTIL
    A @            ( A IS RESULT)
    CR .           ( PRINT RESULT)
;  OK
38 57 GCD2
19  OK
```

Figure 7.16
A program to compute the greatest common divisor
demonstrating the BEGIN. .UNTIL loop.

VOCABULARY

A general familiarity with the following terms and FORTH words is necessary for learning the FORTH language:

And
BEGIN
Body of the loop
Control variable
DO
DO loop
Do until loop
Do while loop
ELSE
Equal to
Equal to zero
Exclusive or
EXIT
False
Greater than
Greater than zero
I
IF
Increment value
Indefinite loop
Initial value
LEAVE
Less than
Less than zero
Limit value
LOOP
Not
Or
REPEAT
THEN
True
Unsigned less than
UNTIL

WHILE

                        EXERCISES

1.   Give results for the following comparison
operations:

          (a) 6 -43 < .
          (b) -1 5 > .
          (c) 10 0 = .
          (d) -4 0< .
          (e) -1 -6 U< .
          (f) 5 0) .
          (g) 3 0= .

2.   Give   results   for   the   following   logical
operations:

          (a) 1 0 AND .
          (b) 0 0 XOR .
          (c) 0 NOT U.
          (d) 111010011100001 001111100010110 XOR .
          (e) 111010011100001 001111100010110 AND .

3. Give the results of the following loops:

          (a) 5 10
              DO
                CR I .
              LOOP

          (b) 3 2
              DO
                CR I DUP + .
              LOOP

          (c) 5 10
              DO
                CR I .
                -1
              +LOOP

4.   What   operation   does   the   following   colon
definition perform?

```
: ??
  DUP
  +-
;
```

5. Write a program to add the integers from 57 to
139 using each of the following constructs:

        (a) DO loop
        (b) BEGIN ..UNTIL loop
        (c) BEGIN..WHILE..REPEAT loop

Chapter 8. DOUBLE PRECISION

Representation

Arithmetic Operations

Stack Manipulation

Mathematical Functions

Comparison Operations

Mixed-Magnitude Operations

Terminal Operations

Constants and Variables

Memory Operations

Vocabulary

Exercises

Many computer applications require a level of
arithmetic precision greater than is available
through the use of 16-bit values. In fact, routine
tabulations commonly involve totals that exceed the
maximum representable single precision value of
32,767. The DOUBLE PRECISION facilities in FORTH
permit calculations involving double length
quantities with the same relative ease with which
single precision calculations can be performed.
This chapter introduces double precision concepts
and covers the FORTH operations that apply to
double precision values. The basic concepts
underlying double precision operations are the same
as for single precision operations. The primary
difference is that alternate FORTH words are used.
Therefore, most topics are presented with a minimum
of introductory material.

REPRESENTATION

A double precision number in FORTH occupies two
16-bit positions in the stack and in memory. In a
double precision number, the left half is called
the "high order" part and the right half is called
the "low order" part. In the stack and in memory,
the high order part of a double precision number is
placed directly above the low order part.
A double precision integer is specified by
placing a period anywhere in the number.
Regardless of where the period is placed the value
stored in the computer is the same. The operation
{D.}, pronounced "d dot," is used to display a
double precision number as follows:

47381. D. 47381 OK

47.381 D. 47381 OK

If the parts of a double precision number are
displayed separately, unusual results are obtained,
as in the following examples:

3 5 D. 327683 OK

327683. . . 5 3 OK

In the first line, two single precision numbers are
routinely entered into the stack and then displayed
as a double precision number. In the second line,
the process is reversed. If the binary bit
patterns are analyzed, then the previous results
make good sense:

HIGH ORDER PART   LOW ORDER PART

Binary 0000000000000101 0000000000000011
            5   3

When a double precision value is displayed, the
high and low order parts are concatenated to form
one long word.
     The leftmost bits of both the high and
low-order parts of a double precision number are
significant when the parts are displayed separately
because they determine the algebraic signs of the
values displayed. As a double precision number,
FORTH determines the algebraic sign of the value
from the leftmost-bit of the high-order part of the
number. Figure 8.1 gives some indication of double
precision bit patterns.
     Another means of entering a double precision
value into the stack is by extending a single
precision value through the use of the following
FORTH operation:

S->D

where the characters are entered without
intervening spaces. When FORTH encounters the word
{S->D}, it removes the single precision value from
the top of the stack, extends it to a double
precision value, and pushes the result back into
the stack. A double precision value is created by
propagating the sign bit of a single precision
value across the high order part of the generated

```
-3 5 D. 393213  OK
-3 5 BINARY D. 101111111111111101  OK
DECIMAL  OK
-3 5 BINARY U. U. 101 111111111111101  OK
DECIMAL  OK
-3 -5 D. -262147  OK
-3 -5 BINARY D. -1000000000000000011  OK
DECIMAL  OK
-3 -5 BINARY CR U. CR U.
1111111111111011
1111111111111101  OK
```

Figure 8.1
Representation of double precision values.

double precision word. Negative double precision values are stored in two's complement form.

ARITHMETIC OPERATIONS

The double precision arithmetic operations in FORTH and their respective operator symbols, recognized as FORTH words are:

OPERATION   FORTH WORD

Double Precision Addition   D+
Double Precision Subtraction   D-
Double Precision Negative   DMINUS

These operations are defined on 32-bit integer values.
The double precision addition operation in FORTH is described symbolically as:

d1 d2 D+ ⟶ sum

where "d1" is the double precision addend and "d2" is the double precision augend. When the word {D+}

is encountered by FORTH, it adds the top two double
precision values in the stack (i.e., d1+d2),
removes them, and places the double precision sum
in the stack. The values can be placed in the
stack directly or may result from a previous
computation. The following examples demonstrate
double precision addition:

        43216. 1. D+ D. 43217 OK

        5000. 60000. -10000. D+ D+ D. 55000 OK

        -35123. 5000. D+ 123. D+ D. -30000 OK

        123 S->D 90000. D+ D. 90123 OK

     The double precision subtraction operation in
FORTH is described symbolically as:

            d1 d2 D-——►difference

where "d1" and "d2" are the double precision
minuend and double precision subtrahend,
respectively. When the word {D-} is encountered by
FORTH, it subtracts the value on the top of the
stack from the value below it (i.e., d1-d2),
removes them, and places the double precision
difference in the stack. As with other FORTH
operations, the values may be placed in the stack
directly or may result from a previous computation.
The following examples demonstrate double precision
subtraction:

        75123. 5123. D- D. 70000 OK

        67887. -2113. D- D. 70000 OK

        90000. -123 S->D D- D. 90123 OK

With double precision subtraction, the subtrahend
is always on the top of the stack. Figure 8.2
depicts a simple FORTH loop that demonstrates a
double precision arithmetic operation.

```
: SUM
  1
  DO
    D+
  LOOP
  CR ." SUM IS " D.
; OK
32768, 50000, 2, 3 SUM
SUM IS 82770  OK
```

Figure 8.2
A FORTH loop demonstrating a double precision
arithmetic operation.

The double precision negation operation in
FORTH changes the sign of the double precision
value on the top of the stack and is described
symbolically as:

d1 DMINUS ⟶ d1

where "d1" is the double precision value on the top
of the stack. The following example demonstrates
the DMINUS operation:

-161289, DMINUS D. 161289 OK

When the word {DMINUS} is encountered by FORTH, it
removes the double precision value from the stack,
takes its two's complement, and places the result
in the stack.
    Double precision multiplication and division
are available as mixed-magnitude operations.

STACK MANIPULATION

The double precision stack manipulation
operations in FORTH and their respective FORTH
words are:

OPERATION	FORTH WORD
Duplicates the top two double precision values on the stack	2DUP
Exchanges the top two double precision values on the stack	2SWAP
Removes the top double precision value from the stack	2DROP
Copies the second double precision value in the stack and puts it on the top	2OVER
Copies the ni-th double precision stack item to the top	2PICK
Rotates the third double precision value in the stack and puts it on the top	2ROT
Rotates the top N double precision stack items	2ROLL

It should be recalled that when visualizing the
stack, the item on the right denotes the top of the
stack.   The ellipsis, i.e., (...), is used to
indicate that items lower in the stack may exist

but they are not restricted to double precision values.
    The   2DUP   operation takes the top double precision value on the stack, duplicates it, and pushes the duplicated value into the stack. The stack contents before and after the operation are:

              Operation: 2DUP
              Stack before: ...d1
              Stack after: ...d1 d1

    The   2SWAP operation exchanges the top two double   precision values on the stack without disturbing the other stack values.   The stack contents before and after the 2SWAP operation are:

              Operation: 2SWAP
              Stack before: ...d1 d2
              Stack after: ...d2 d1

    The   2DROP   operation   removes   the double precision value on the top of the stack so that all of the values below it are moved up. The stack contents before and after the execution of the 2DROP operation are:

              Operation: 2DROP
              Stack before: ...d1 d2
              Stack after: ...d1

    The 2OVER operation takes the second double precision value in the stack, duplicates it, and pushes the duplicated value into the stack. The stack contents before and after the execution of the 2OVER operation are:

              Operation: 2OVER
              Stack before: ...d1 d2
              Stack after: ...d1 d2 d1

    The 2PICK operation copies a stack entry to the top of the stack without disturbing the relative order of the values.   This operation uses the

single precision number on the top of the stack to
determine the "depth" of the pick operation. The
stack contents before and after the execution of
the 2PICK operation are:

        Operation: 2PICK
        Stack before: d1...d(i-1) di d(i+1)...dK n
        Stack after: d1...d(i-1) di d(i+1)...dK di

where i=K-n+1.   The value on the top of the stack
that determines the depth of the 2PICK operation is
removed. The statement {1 2PICK} is the same as the
2DUP operation, and the statement {2 2PICK} is the
same as the 2OVER operation.
    The 2ROT operation works with the top three
double precision values in the stack. The double
precision value that is third from the top is
rotated to the top, and the two values above it are
pushed down.   The stack contents before and after
the execution of the 2ROT operation are:

        Operation: 2ROT
        Stack before: ...d1 d2 d3
        Stack after: ...d2 d3 d1

    The 2ROLL operation is similar to the 2ROT
operation, but uses the single precision value on
the top of the stack to determine the "depth" of
the roll.   The statement {3 2ROLL} is the same as
the 2ROT operation. The stack before and after the
execution of the 2ROLL operation are:

        Operation: 2ROLL
        Stack before: d1...d(i-1) di d(i+1)...dK n
        Stack after: d1...d(i-1) d(i+1)...dK di

where i=K-n+1.   The value on the top of the stack
that determines the depth of the roll is removed.
    Figure 8.3 gives several examples of double
precision stack manipulation operations.   The
examples are routine cases to demonstrate the
manner in which the double precision stack
manipulation operations function.

```
32768. 2DUP D. D. 32768 32768  OK
40000. 50000. 2SWAP D. D. 40000 50000  OK
40000. 50000. 2DROP D. 40000  OK
65535. -14. 2OVER D. D. D. 65535 -14 65535  OK
-7. 3. 9. 2ROT D. D. D. -7 9 3  OK
-17. 23. 6. 10. 4 2ROLL CR D. D. D. D.
-17 10 6 23  OK
```

Figure 8.3
Examples of stack manipulation operations.

MATHEMATICAL FUNCTIONS

The double precision mathematical functions in
FORTH complement the single precision functions and
have the same mathematical meaning. The following
double precision mathematical functions are
included in FORTH:

FUNCTION   FORTH WORD

Double precision absolute value   DABS
Double precision maximum   DMAX
Double precision minimum   DMIN
Double precision sign   D+-

All double precision mathematical functions are
defined on double precision values held in the
stack.
     The double precision absolute value function in
FORTH is described symbolically as:

d1 DABS   d2

where d2 is a positive double precision integer.
When the word {DABS} is encountered by FORTH, it
removes the top double precision stack entry,
computes its absolute value, and places the result
in the stack. The following examples demonstrate

the absolute value function:

        -171264. DABS D. 171264 OK

        41390. DABS D. 41390 OK

    The double precision maximum function in FORTH
is described symbolically as:

            d1 d2 DMAX——▶d3

where d3 is the maximum of d1 and d2. The DMAX
function removes the top two double precision
values from the stack, computes the value that is
mathematically larger, and places the result in the
stack.   The following examples demonstrate the
maximum function:

        -63152. -59004. DMAX D. -59004 OK

        35190. -14. DMAX D. 35190 OK

    The double precision minimum function in FORTH
is described symbolically as:

            d1 d2 DMIN——▶d3

where d3 is the minimum of d1 and d2. The DMIN
function removes the top two double precision
values from the stack, computes the value that is
mathematically smaller, and places the result back
in the stack.   The following examples demonstrate
the minimum function:

        -63152. -59004. DMIN D. -63152 OK

        35190. -14. DMIN D. -14 OK

    The double precision sign function applies the
arithmetic sign of the single precision value on
the top of the stack to the double precision value
below it.   This function is described symbolically
as:

$$d1 \ n \ D+- \longrightarrow d2$$

where d2=sign(n)*d1. The values d1 and n are
removed from the stack and the result is placed in
the   stack   as   demonstrated   in   the   following
examples:

50000. -1 D+- D. -50000 OK

-50000. -1 D+- D. 50000 OK

-50000. 1 D+- D. -50000 OK

        The   mixed-mode   operations on single and double
precision   values   constitute   other   mathematical
functions. They are covered in a separate section.

COMPARISON OPERATIONS

        The   double   precision   comparison operations in
FORTH   and   their   respective   operator   symbols,
recognized as FORTH words are:

OPERATION	FORTH WORD
Less than	D<
Greater than	D>
Equal to	D=
Equal to zero	D0=
Unsigned less than	DU<

These operations are defined on 32-bit integer
values.
        The   double   precision   less   than   operation in
FORTH is described symbolically as:

$$d1 \ d2 \ D< \longrightarrow flag$$

where "d1" is the leftmost operand and "d2" is the
rightmost operand in the mathematical expression
d1<d2.   The operands are entered in the same order

as they would be entered in ordinary mathematical
notation. When FORTH encounters the word {D<}, the
top two double precision values are removed from
the stack and the comparison operation (i.e.,
d1<d2) is performed. If the value of d1 is less
than the value of d2, then a "true" value of 1 is
pushed into the stack. Otherwise, a "false" value
of 0 is pushed into the stack. The following
examples demonstrate the double precision less than
operation:

        40000. 50000. D< . 1 OK

        50000. 40000. D< . 0 OK

        -173. 0. D< . 1 OK

     The double precision greater than operation in
FORTH is described symbolically as:

                d1 d2 D) —► flag

where "d1" is the leftmost operand and "d2" is the
rightmost operand in the mathematical expression
d1>d2. The operands are entered in the same order
as they would be entered in ordinary mathematical
notation. When FORTH encounters the word {D>}, the
top two double precision values are removed from
the stack and the comparison operation (i.e.,
d1>d2) is performed. If the value of d1 is greater
than the value of d2, then a "true" value of 1 is
pushed into the stack. Otherwise, a "false" value
of 0 is pushed into the stack. The following
examples demonstrate the double precision greater
than operation:

        0. -173. D) . 1 OK

        69145. 32961. D) . 1 OK

        9999. 89423. D) . 0 OK

     The double precision equal to operation in

FORTH is described symbolically as:

$$d1 \quad d2 \quad D= \longrightarrow flag$$

where "d1" is the leftmost operand and "d2" is the rightmost operand in the mathematical expression d1=d2. The operands are entered in the same order as they would be entered in ordinary mathematical notation. When FORTH encounters the word {D=}, the top two double precision values are removed from the stack and the equal to operation (i.e., d1=d2) is performed. If the value of d1 is equal to the value of d2, then a "true" value of 1 is pushed into the stack. Otherwise, a "false" value of 0 is pushed into the stack. The following examples demonstrate the double precision equal to operation:

       72689. 72689. D= . 1 OK

       -4365. 4365. D= . 0 OK

       -0. 0. D= . 1 OK

     The double precision equal to zero operation in FORTH is described symbolically as:

$$d \quad D0= \longrightarrow flag$$

where "d" is a double precision value to be compared with zero, as in the mathematical expression d=0. When FORTH encounters the word {D0=}, the double precision value on the top of the stack is removed and compared with zero. If the value of d is equal to zero, then a "true" value of 1 is pushed into the stack. Otherwise, a "false" value of 0 is pushed into the stack. The following examples demonstrate the double precision equal to zero operation:

       95222. D0= . 0 OK

       0. D0= . 1 OK

<u>0 0 DO= . 1 OK</u>

The double precision unsigned less than operation in FORTH is described symbolically as:

ud1 ud2 DU< ──▶ flag

where "ud1" is the leftmost operand and "ud2" is the rightmost operand in the mathematical expression ud1<ud2. This operation is the same as {D<} except that the sign bit of the operands is interpreted as a data bit. The operands are entered in the same order as they would be entered in ordinary mathematical notation. When FORTH encounters the word {DU<}, the two double precision values are removed from the stack and the comparison operation (i.e., ud1<ud2) is performed. If the value of ud1 is less than the value of ud2, then a "true" value of 1 is pushed into the stack. Otherwise, a "false" value of 0 is pushed into the stack. The following examples demonstrate the double precision unsigned less than operation:

<u>40000. 50000. DU< . 1 OK</u>

<u>40000. -50000. DU< . 1 OK</u>

<u>-50000. -40000. DU< . 1 OK</u>

All double precision comparison operations yield single precision "flag" values that can be used as operands in logical operations.

MIXED MAGNITUDE OPERATIONS

Mixed magnitude operations provide a means of utilizing the multiplicative operations in computer integer arithmetic. In general, the product of two single precision integers yields a double precision product and the division of a double precision dividend by a single precision divisor yields a

single precision quotient and a single precision
remainder.   Mixed-magnitude multiplication in
FORTH is described symbolically as:

$$n1 \quad n2 \quad M* \longrightarrow d$$

where "n1" and "n2" are the single precision
multiplier and multiplicand, respectively, and "d"
is the double precision product. When the word
{M*} is encountered by FORTH, it removes the top
two single precision values from the stack,
multiplies them forming a double precision product
(i.e., n1*n2), and pushes the result into the stack
as a double precision value. The following example
demonstrates mixed-magnitude multiplication:

    20000 30000 M* D. 600000000 OK

    Mixed-magnitude division in FORTH is described
symbolically as:

$$d \quad n1 \quad M/ \longrightarrow n2 \quad n3$$

where "d" is the double precision dividend, "n1" is
the single precision divisor, "n2" is the single
precision remainder, and "n3" is the single
precision quotient.   When the word {M/} is
encountered by FORTH, it removes the single
precision value from the top of the stack and the
double precision value below it. The division
operation (i.e., d/n1) is performed, and the
remainder (i.e., n2) and the quotient (i.e., n3)
are pushed into the stack. The following example
demonstrates mixed-magnitude division:

    600000001. 20000 M/ . . 30000 1 OK

    The unsigned mixed-magnitude multiplication
operation in FORTH is described symbolically as:

$$u1 \quad u2 \quad U* \longrightarrow ud$$

where "u1" and "u2" are the unsigned single

precision   multiplier   and   multiplicand,
respectively,   and   "ud"   is   the   unsigned   double
precision   product.   When FORTH encounters the word
{U*},   the   top   two   single   precision   values   are
removed   from   the   top   of the stack and multiplied
together   (i.e.,   u1*u2)   using   all 16 bits of each
operand   with   the   sign   bit   interpreted as a data
bit.   The   unsigned   double   precision   result   is
pushed   into   the   stack.   The   following   example
demonstrates   unsigned   mixed-magnitude
multiplication:

<u>   -5 -3 U* D. -524273   OK</u>

    The   unsigned mixed-magnitude division operation
in FORTH is described symbolically as:

        ud u1 U/——►u2 u3

where   "ud"   is   the   unsigned   double   precision
dividend,   "u1"   is   the   unsigned   single precision
divisor,   "u2"   is   the   unsigned   single   precision
remainder,   and   "u3"   is   the   unsigned   single
precision   quotient.   When   the   word   {U/}   is
encountered   by FORTH, it removes the top two values
from   the   stack.   The   first   value which is on the
top   of   the   stack is the unsigned single precision
divisor   and   the   value   below   it   is the unsigned
double   precision   dividend.   The division operation
(i.e.,   ud/u1)   is   executed and the unsigned single
precision   remainder   and   quotient   are pushed into
the   stack.   The   following example demonstrates the
unsigned mixed-magnitude division operation:

<u>   -600000001. -30000 U/ U. U. 43546 32991   OK</u>

    The   unsigned   mixed-magnitude   divide   modulus
operation in FORTH is described symbolically as:

        ud1 u2 M/MOD—►u3 ud4

where   "ud1"   is   the   unsigned   double   precision
dividend,   "u2"   is   the   unsigned   single precision

divisor, "u3" is the unsigned single precision
remainder, and "ud4" is the unsigned double
precision quotient. When FORTH encounters the word
{M/MOD}, the single precision divisor and double
precision dividend are removed from the stack and
the division operation (i.e., ud1/u2) is executed.
The unsigned single precision remainder and the
unsigned double precision quotient are pushed into
the stack. The following example demonstrates this
operation:

-600000001. -30000 M/MOD D. U. 103978 5087   OK

In general, the unsigned values selected as
operands for mixed-magnitude operations permit the
full word capability to be used for applications
that require it.

TERMINAL OPERATIONS

The D-DOT OPERATION represented by the word
{D.} outputs a double precision value to the
printer or display. This operation was presented
earlier in this chapter. The d-dot operation is
described symbolically as:

d D.

where "d" is the double precision value to be
displayed, which is always placed on the output
medium with a trailing space character. When the
word {D.} is encountered by FORTH, the double
precision value on the top of the stack is removed
and displayed. The d-dot operation displays a
negative number in true form with a preceding minus
sign. Positive values are displayed without a
preceding plus sign. The value is converted from
internal binary to external form according to the
number base stored in BASE.
The D-DOT-R OPERATION displays a double
precision value while permitting the programmer to
specify a field width. The d-dot-r operation uses
the FORTH word {D.R} as an operator symbol and is

described symbolically as:

d width D.R

where "d" is the double precision value to be
displayed and "width" is a single precision value
representing the field width. Both values are in
the stack with the width on top and the double
precision value below it. When the word {D.R} is
encountered by FORTH, both values are removed from
the stack and the output operation is performed.
The output value is always right justified in the
field. The d-dot-r operation adheres to the same
output conversion rules as the d-dot operation.

CONSTANTS AND VARIABLES

A double precision constant is defined in FORTH
with a statement of the form:

value 2CONSTANT name

where "value" is the value of the double precision
constant and "name" is the name by which it is
referenced. The following examples demonstrate the
definition and use of a double precision constant:

75301. 2CONSTANT LMT   OK

LMT D. 75301   OK

The word {2CONSTANT} is an executable operation in
FORTH. When it is encountered by FORTH, the double
precision value on the top of the stack is used as
the value of the double precision constant. The
word following 2CONSTANT is the name of the
constant, and the double precision value on the top
of the stack is removed during the execution of the
operation.
A double precison constant is referenced by
using its name, as demonstrated in the preceding
example. When the name of a double precision

constant is encountered by FORTH, the value of the
double precision constant is pushed into the stack.
    A double precision variable is defined in FORTH
with a statement of the form:

                value 2VARIABLE name

where "value" is the initial value of the double
precision variable and "name" is the name by which
it is referenced. The following examples
demonstrate the definition of a variable:

        -131294. 2VARIABLE CTL   OK

        0. 2VARIABLE DSUM   OK

        5. 2VARIABLE DFIVE   OK

The word 2VARIABLE is an executable operation in
FORTH that uses the double precision value on the
top of the stack as the initial value of the double
precision variable. When the word 2VARIABLE is
encountered by FORTH, the double precision value on
the top of the stack is removed as the initial
value of the variable and the word following
2VARIABLE is the name of the variable.
    Each time the word 2VARIABLE is encountered by
FORTH, a new double precision variable is defined.
Therefore, the word should not be used to change
the value of a variable. The FORTH word
{2VARIABLE} should only be used to declare a
variable initially.
    When the name of a double precision variable is
encountered by FORTH, the address of the double
precision variable is placed on the stack. The
address is used with the double precision store and
fetch operations.

                    MEMORY OPERATIONS

    The double precision fetch operation uses the
value on the top of the stack as the address of a

double   precision   value   and   is   described
symbolically as:

$$addr\ 2@ \longrightarrow d$$

where "addr" is a memory address and "d" is the
double precision value stored at the specified
address.   The following examples demonstrate the
double precision fetch operation:

    50000. 2VARIABLE PAY   OK

    PAY 2@ D. 50000   OK

    5000. 2CONSTANT RAISE   OK

    RAISE PAY 2@ D+ D. 55000   OK

When the word {2@} is encountered by FORTH, it
removes the single precision value on the top of
the   stack   interpreting   the   value as an address.
The double precision value at the specified address
location is "fetched" from memory and pushed into
the stack.
     The double precision fetch operation should not
be used with a double precision constant because
reference to the name of a constant always yields
the value of the constant and not its memory
address.
     The double precision store operation is used to
place a double precision value from the stack into
memory at a specified address and is described
symbolically as:

$$d\ addr\ 2!$$

where "d" is the double precision value to be
placed in memory and "addr" is the memory address
where the value should be placed. The address is
on the top of the stack and the double precision
value is directly below it. When the word {2!} is
encountered by FORTH, the top two stack entries -
one   for the address and one for the double

precision value - are removed from the stack and
the double precision store operation is performed.
The following statements demonstrate the double
precision store operation:

    69999. 2VARIABLE TOP   OK

    70000. TOP 2!   OK

    TOP 2@ D. 70000   OK

When a double precision store operation to a memory
location is performed, the previous contents of
that location are lost.
    As with the double precision fetch operation,
the double precision store operation should not be
used with a double precision constant because a
reference to the name of a double precision
constant yields the value of the constant and not
its memory address. Figure 8.4 gives several
examples of the definition and use of double
precision variables and the double precision fetch
and store operations.

        50000. 2VARIABLE DA   OK
        100000. 2VARIABLE DB   OK
        : EXCH
          DA 2@ DB 2@
          2SWAP DB 2! DA 2!
        ;   OK
        EXCH   OK
        DA 2@ D. 100000   OK
        DB 2@ D. 50000   OK

Figure 8.4
A set of double precision operations that exchange the
values of double precision variables DA and DB.

VOCABULARY

A general familiarity with the following terms
and FORTH words is necessary for learning the FORTH
language:

    2!
    2@
    2CONSTANT
    2DROP
    2DUP
    2OVER
    2PICK
    2ROLL
    2ROT
    2SWAP
    2VARIABLE
    D.
    D+
    D-
    D+-
    D<
    D>
    D=
    D0=
    DABS
    DMAX
    DMIN
    DMINUS
    Double-precision value
    D.R
    DU<
    M*
    M/
    M/MOD
    Mixed-magnitude operation
    S->D
    U*
    U/

EXERCISES

Develop colon definitions for the following double-precision functions:

1. Double plus store

   Operation: D+!
   Stack before: ... d addr
   Stack after: ...
   Result: d is added to the double
           precision value at addr

2. Double one plus store

   Operation: D1+!
   Stack before: ... addr
   Stack after: ...
   Result: 1 is added to the double
           precision value at addr

3. Double one minus store

   Operation: D1-!
   Stack before: ... addr
   Stack after: ...
   Result: 1 is subtracted from the
           double precision value at
           addr

4. Double one plus

   Operation: D1+
   Stack before: ... d1
   Stack after: ... d2
   Result: d2   d1+1

5. Double one minus

   Operation: D1-
   Stack before: ... d1
   Stack after: ... d2
   Result: d2   d1-1

6. Double two plus

    Operation: D2+
    Stack before: ... d1
    Stack after: ... d2
    Result: d2   d1+2

7. Double two minus

    Operation: D2-
    Stack before: ... d1
    Stack after: ... d2
    Result: d2   d1-2

Chapter 9. INFORMATION MANAGEMENT

Memory Organization

Allocation

Disk Input and Output

Program Management

Keyboard Operations

Character Movement

Output Formatting and Conversion

Vocabulary

Exercises

Information in FORTH is organized around the concept of a SCREEN, which is a 1024-byte block of memory. Disk storage is divided into screens and the FORTH system contains a fixed number of screen-sized buffers for working memory and for disk input/output. The word "screen" corresponds to a virtual display screen consisting of sixteen 64-character lines. Programs are also organized into screens and language features are available for loading and executing screens on a static or dynamic basis.

MEMORY ORGANIZATION

The FORTH system contains a fixed number of screen buffers that are managed on a dynamic basis. When the user requests memory by employing one of several well-defined methods, a screen buffer is assigned on a "least recently used" basis. If, for example, the assigned buffer holds a disk input/output screen that has been updated, the current buffer contents are rewritten to disk storage before the screen buffer is reassigned.

The number of screen buffers in a particular FORTH system is implementation-dependent and is assigned by default. This number can be changed, providing a tradeoff between buffer space and dictionary space.

ALLOCATION

A screen buffer can be allocated explicitly or implicitly. Explicit allocation is made with the BUFFER operation. Implicit allocation is made with the LOAD or BLOCK operations. Explicit screen buffer allocation is covered here.

The BUFFER operation is described symbolically as:

n BUFFER→addr

where "n" is a screen number and "addr" is a buffer
address.   When FORTH encounters the word {BUFFER},
it removes the screen number from the top of the
stack and assigns a buffer to it. If the screen
buffer has been marked for updating, the contents
of the buffer are written to disk. The address of
the buffer is returned by pushing it into the
stack.   The allocated buffer can then be used as a
1024-byte storage area in memory.

DISK INPUT AND OUTPUT

A screen is read from disk to memory with the
BLOCK operation which takes the following form:

$$n\ BLOCK \longrightarrow addr$$

where "n" is a screen number and "addr" is a buffer
address.   When FORTH encounters the word {BLOCK},
it removes the screen number from the top of the
stack and assigns a buffer to it on a least
recently used basis. If the screen buffer has been
marked for updating, the contents of the buffer are
written to disk. Then, the contents of disk screen
numbered "n" are read into the assigned screen
buffer in memory from disk and its address is
pushed into the stack. The BLOCK operation employs
implicit screen buffer allocation since allocation
is performed in support of a distinct FORTH
operation.   A screen buffer is marked for
updating with the UPDATE operation.   When FORTH
encounters the word {UPDATE}, the screen buffer
last referenced is marked for updating.
The contents of a screen buffer that have been
marked for updating are written to disk under two
circumstances:

o The screen buffer is re-allocated
o The SAVE-BUFFERS operation is executed

When the word {SAVE-BUFFERS} is encountered by
FORTH, all screen buffers marked for updating are

written to disk. The FORTH word {SAVE-BUFFERS} is synonymous with the word {FLUSH}, which is used in some FORTH systems.

The EMPTY-BUFFERS operation is used to mark all screen buffers as empty. When a subsequent EMPTY-BUFFERS operation is encountered by FORTH, the effect of the UPDATE operation is nullified so that the contents of the screen buffers are not written to disk.

PROGRAM MANAGEMENT

Programs in FORTH can be entered into the system via the keyboard or through the use of a disk screen. From the keyboard, statements are keyed in the execution or definition mode and FORTH responds immediately. This topic was covered earlier.

Another facility for program management is to use a screen editor to construct a display screen containing FORTH statements and to store it on disk as a screen. A disk screen can be loaded for execution and FORTH responds as though the statements were entered from the keyboard.

The LOAD operation in FORTH is described symbolically as:

n LOAD

where "n" is the number of a disk screen. When the word {LOAD} is encountered by FORTH, the screen number is removed from the stack. A screen buffer is implicitly assigned, as covered previously, and the disk screen is read in. FORTH treats the contents of the screen buffer as though it were entered via the keyboard. LOAD operations can be nested, which means that one disk screen may contain another LOAD operation, and so forth.

The NEXT SCREEN operation is described symbolically as:

-->

which commands FORTH to continue interpretation
with the next disk screen in numerical sequence.
    The   interpretation   of   a   screen   can   be
terminated with the following FORTH word:

                          ;S

allowing   the remainder of the screen to be used for
comments.
    When   FORTH encounters the word {;S} or comes to
the   end of a screen, interpretive execution resumes
with   the   FORTH operation immediately following the
last LOAD operation that was executed. Thus, in
effect, a "return" is made to the "calling screen."
    The LIST operation is used to display the
contents of a screen and is described symbolically
as:

                        n LIST

where   "n" is the screen number of the text to be
displayed.   If the specified screen is in memory,
it   is   displayed without disk input.   If the
specified   screen   is not in memory, a screen buffer
is   allocated   and the specified screen is read into
memory and displayed.
    The   SCR   command returns the address of a
variable containing the number of the screen most
recently   listed.   This operation is described
symbolically as:

                    SCR—►addr

where   "addr" is the address of the variable that
contains   the screen number. The address would then
be   followed with a fetch operation, such as {SCR
@}, to obtain the screen number. This operation
would   normally be used when listing several screens
in succession under program control or when the
user   simply forgot the number of the screen that he
or   she most recently listed. In some versions of
FORTH,   the operation SCR is also used with editor

related commands.

KEYBOARD OPERATIONS

Through the use of keyboard operations, strings of characters can be entered directly into memory and can be displayed from memory.

The EXPECT operation is used for data entry and is described symbolically as:

addr n EXPECT

where "addr" is the beginning memory address and "n" is the number of characters to be transmitted. When FORTH encounters the word {EXPECT}, characters entered from the keyboard are placed in consecutive byte locations in memory until "n" characters or the carriage return is entered. Two null characters are appended to the end of the string, and sufficient space should be available in the memory buffer for these characters.

The TYPE operation is used to display character strings from memory and is described symbolically as:

addr n TYPE

where "addr" is the beginning memory address and "n" is the character count. When FORTH encounters the word {TYPE}, "n" characters from consecutive memory locations starting with the specified address are displayed. Figure 9.1 demonstrates the use of the BUFFER, EXPECT, and TYPE operations.

The KEY operation permits the ASCII code of a character entered at the keyboard to be entered into the stack. This operation is described symbolically as:

KEY → c

where "c" is the ASCII code of the character entered. When FORTH encounters the word {KEY}, it

```
0 VARIABLE STRING   OK
: IN-OUT
  50 BUFFER
  STRING !
  CR ." ENTER 5 CHARACTERS "
  STRING @ 5 EXPECT
  CR ." YOU ENTERED: "
  STRING @ 5 TYPE
  CR ." END OF IN-OUT "
;  OK
IN-OUT
ENTER 5 CHARACTERS FORTH
YOU ENTERED: FORTH
END OF IN-OUT   OK
```

Figure 9.1
A sample colon definition demonstrating the
BUFFER, EXPECT, and TYPE operations.

waits until a character is entered from the keyboard and then pushes its ASCII code into the stack.

The EMIT operation reverses the effect of the key operation by taking an ASCII code from the stack and displaying its corresponding character. This operation is described symbolically as:

c EMIT

where "c" is the ASCII code to be displayed. When FORTH encounters the word {EMIT}, the ASCII code on the top of the stack is removed and the corresponding character is displayed.

The ?TERMINAL operation is used to break a continuous operation, such as a listing, and is described symbolically as:

?TERMINAL → flag

where "flag" is either a 1 or a 0. When FORTH

encounters the word {?TERMINAL}, it tests whether a
key has been struck. If a key has been struck, a
value of 1 is pushed into the stack. Otherwise, a
value of 0 is pushed into the stack.

CHARACTER MOVEMENT

Character movement operations in FORTH permit
character data to be moved from one area of memory
to another. Also included in the set of operations
are a variety of "utility" operations that
facilitate FORTH programming.

The character movement operations in FORTH are
summarized as follows:

DESCRIPTION	FORTH WORD
Store 8 bits	C!
Fetch 8 bits	C@
Character movement	CMOVE
Suppress trailing blanks	-TRAILING
Fill memory with specified byte	FILL
Fill memory with blanks	BLANKS
Move 16-bit memory cells	MOVE

When a byte is specified as an operand, it occupies
the low-order byte position of a stack entry. The
high-order bits of that stack entry are not used.

The STORE BYTE operation in FORTH is described
symbolically as:

byte addr C!

where "byte" is the data to be stored and "addr" is
the memory address. When FORTH encounters the word
{C!}, the top two values are removed from the
stack. The topmost entry is the memory address and
the entry below it contains the byte to be stored.
This FORTH operation is pronounced "c-store."

Normally, the specified byte will contain the ASCII code of a character.

The FETCH BYTE operation in FORTH is described symbolically as:

$$addr \; C@ \longrightarrow byte$$

where "addr" is a memory address and "byte" is the data that has been fetched. When FORTH encounters the word {C@}, the top entry is removed from the stack. This is the memory address. A fetch operation is made to the specified byte address in memory and a stack entry is created. The 8 bits fetched occupy the low- order position of the stack entry, which is pushed into the stack. This FORTH operation is pronounced "c-fetch." Normally, the specified byte will contain the ASCII code of a character.

The CHARACTER MOVE operation in FORTH is used to move a block of characters from one area of memory to another. This operation is described symbolically as:

$$addr1 \; addr2 \; n \; CMOVE$$

where "addr1" and "addr2" are the from and to memory addresses, respectively, and "n" is the number of character positions (i.e., byte locations) to be moved. When FORTH encounters the word {CMOVE}, the top three entries are removed from the stack representing addr1, addr2, and n, in that order, from the top. The character movement is performed from addr1 to addr2 starting with the lower memory address. If n is less than or equal to zero, no movement is performed.

The SUPPRESS TRAILING BLANKS operation eliminates trailing blanks by adjusting the character count of a string reference. This operation is described symbolically as:

$$addr \; n1 \; -TRAILING \longrightarrow addr \; n2$$

where "addr" is the memory address of the character

string and "n1" is the length of the string. When
FORTH encounters the word {-TRAILING}, it removes
the top two values from the stack, representing the
length and address, respectively. Trailing blanks
are eliminated and the old address and the new
character count "n2" are pushed into the stack.
     The FILL operation places a specified character
into each byte location of an area of memory. This
operation is described symbolically as:

                  addr n byte FILL

where "addr" is the starting address, "n" is the
number of byte locations to be filled, and "byte"
is the quantity to be placed in each byte location.
Normally, byte is an ASCII code of a character.
When FORTH encounters the word {FILL}, the top
three values are removed from the stack,
representing byte, n, and addr going from the top
downwards. The FILL operation is performed from
the starting address upwards in memory. If n is
less than or equal to zero, no fill operation is
performed.
     Figure 9.2 demonstrates the FILL, CMOVE, and
-TRAILING operations.
     The BLANKS operation in FORTH fills an area of
memory with blanks and is described symbolically
as:

                  addr n BLANKS

where "addr" is the starting address and "n" is the
number of byte locations to be filled with a blank
character.   When FORTH encounters the word
{BLANKS}, the top two values are removed from the
stack, representing the count and starting address,
respectively. The specified area of memory is
filled from the starting address upwards with the
ASCII code for the blank character. If n is less
than or equal to zero, no memory locations are
filled with a blank.

```
0 VARIABLE FROM  OK
0 VARIABLE TO  OK
: CMOVEMENT
  60 BUFFER
  FROM !
  70 BUFFER
  TO !
  FROM @ 50 192 FILL
  CR ." ENTER 5 LETTERS AND 5 SPACES "
  FROM @ 10 EXPECT
  FROM @ TO @ 10 CMOVE
  TO @ 10 -TRAILING
  CR ." THE RESULT IS: "
  TYPE
  CR ." END OF CMOVEMENT "
;  OK
CMOVEMENT
ENTER 5 LETTERS AND 5 SPACES FORTH
THE RESULT IS: FORTH
END OF CMOVEMENT  OK
```

Figure 9.2
Example of character movement demonstrating the
FILL, CMOVE, and -TRAILING operations.

The MOVE operation in FORTH moves a specified number of 16-bit memory cells from one area of memory to another. This operation is described symbolically as:

$$addr1 \quad addr2 \quad n \quad MOVE$$

where "addr1" and "addr2" are the from and to memory addresses, respectively, and "n" is the number of 16-bit memory cells to be moved. When FORTH encounters the word {MOVE}, the top three values, representing the count, to address, and from address, going downwards, are removed from the stack. The 16-bit memory cells are moved starting with the specified address upwards. If n is less than or equal to zero, no movement is performed.

OUTPUT FORMATTING AND CONVERSION

The FORTH language contains an output formatting facility to specify the conversion of a double-precision number into an ASCII character string. FORTH incorporates the following words that deal exclusively with output formatting:

<# # #S HOLD SIGN #>

Looking at output formatting conceptually, the word {<#} puts the system into the output formatting mode and the word {#>} is usd to exit from the output formatting mode. The words {#}, {#S}, {HOLD}, and {SIGN} can only be used between <# and #>.

Output formatting is designed around double precision numbers because most business applications require more significant digits than are available with sixteen-bit single precision values. For example, the largest single precision representable number with dollars and cents would be $327.67.

Figure 9.3 gives a general-purpose double precision output formatting routine that can be used with a variety of business applications. It is explained in the following paragraphs.

Output formatting proceeds from right to left and essentially operates by dividing the number by the base and converting the remainder to an ASCII code. The formatting procedures utilize an unsigned double precision number. The steps in the definition {$.} are explained as follows:

a. {2DUP DABS} saves the algebraic sign and creates a positive value.

b. {<#} puts the system into the output formatting mode.

c. {# #} converts the cents portion of the word

placing the ASCII digits in the text string.

d. {46 HOLD} puts the ASCII code for the decimal point into the text string.

e. {#S} converts the remainder of the number.

f. {SIGN DROP} puts the ASCII code for the minus into the text string if the original value was negative. This operation uses only the high-order part so the low order part is dropped.

g. {36 HOLD} puts the ASCII code for the dollar sign into the text string.

h. {#)} exits the output formatting mode and leaves the addr and count on the stack for the TYPE operation

i. {TYPE SPACE} displays the result.

Since the operation {#)} does in fact put the address and character count of the text string in

```
: $.              ( OUTPUT FORMATTING )
   2DUP DABS      ( SET UP DATA        )
   (#             ( ENTER FORMAT MODE )
     # #          ( CONVERT CENTS      )
     46 HOLD      ( PUT IN DEC POINT   )
     #S           ( CONVERT DOLLARS    )
     SIGN DROP    ( PUT IN SIGN        )
     36 HOLD      ( PUT IN $           )
   #)             ( EXIT FORMAT MODE   )
   TYPE SPACE     ( DISPLAY RESULT     )
;  OK
12345. $. $123.45  OK
-6738124. $. $-67381.24  OK
```

Figure 9.3
General purpose output formatting routine.

the   stack, it can be followed by any FORTH
operation that deals with character movement, such
as the CMOVE or TYPE operations.
    There is relatively little need to convert
numbers from ASCII code to internal binary since
numerical data can be entered into the stack from
the keyboard.   However, turnkey systems frequently
require data verification, so that FORTH operations
are also available for input conversion.
    The (NUMBER) operation in FORTH is used to
convert ASCII text into a number. This operation
is described symbolically as:

            d1 addr1 (NUMBER) ⟶ d2 addr2

where "d1" is a double precision number into which
the   new value is accumulated, "addr1" is the
address of the ASCII text, "d2" is the new double
precision value, and "addr2" is the address of the
first unconvertable digit.   When FORTH encounters
the   word {(NUMBER)}, it removes the address from
the top of the stack and the double precision value
below it.   The ASCII text is converted to binary
starting with the specified address plus one (i.e.,
addr1+1)   and   accumulated into the specified
double-precision value (i.e., d1).   The double
precision result is pushed into the stack followed
by the address in memory of the first unconvertable
character in the ASCII text string. Figure 9.4
gives an example of the use of the (NUMBER)
operation.

```
0 VARIABLE LOC   OK
: TEST-NUM
  50 BUFFER                ( GET STORAGE)
  LOC !                    ( SAVE ADDRESS)
  LOC @ 1 + 8 EXPECT   ( ASCII DATA)
  0.                       ( ACCUMULATOR)
  LOC @ (NUMBER)       ( CONVERT)
  DROP                     ( DROP ADDRESS)
  CR ." NUMBER IS: "
  D.                       ( CONVERTED VALUE)
;   OK
TEST-NUM 2376914K
NUMBER IS: 2376914   OK
```

Figure 9.4
Example of input conversion.

VOCABULARY

A general familiarity with the following terms
and FORTH words is necessary for learning the FORTH
language:

```
#
#)
#S
-->
(#
;S
?TERMINAL
-TRAILING
BLANKS
BLOCK
BUFFER
C@
C!
CMOVE
EMIT
EMPTY-BUFFERS
EXPECT
```

    Explicit allocation
    FILL
    HOLD
    Implicit allocation
    KEY
    Least recently used
    LIST
    LOAD
    MOVE
    (NUMBER)
    SAVE-BUFFERS
    SCR
    Screen
    SIGN
    TYPE
    UPDATE

EXERCISES

1.   Write a FORTH statement to place blank
characters in 100 byte locations starting with the
address stored in variable START.

2. Write a FORTH statement to move 1000 bytes from
hex location 6FC to hex location FF3.

3. Starting at decimal location 2000 is an 11
character message.   Give a FORTH statement to have
the message displayed.

4. Write a FORTH statement to place the letter "A"
in byte location 10111 (binary).

5.   Write a FORTH program to obtain a buffer
containing at least 100 bytes. Place the character
"@" in odd byte locations and the character "+" in
even byte locations. Then display the result as 10
rows of 10 characters.

REFERENCES

[1] Crazon, H.G., "The elements of single-chip microcomputer architecture," COMPUTER, Volume 13, Number 10 (October, 1980), pp. 27-41.

[2] Engineering Research Associates, High-Speed Computing Devices, McGraw-Hill Book Company, New York, 1950.

[3] FORTH-79, FORTH Interest Group, 1980. (P.O. Box 1105, San Carlos, California 94070)

[4] FORTH Ver. 1.7: Language Manual And User's Guide, Cap'n Software, 1980.

[5] Harris, K., "FORTH Extensibility: Or How to Write a Compiler in 25 Words or Less," Byte (August, 1980), pp. 164-184.

[6] Hilburn, J.L. and P.M. Julich, Microcomputers/Microprocessors: Hardware, Software, and Applications, Prentice-Hall, Inc., Englewood Cliffs, New Jersey, 1976.

[7] Holder, C.L., "Small businesses use floppy disk word processing," Small Systems World (September, 1980), pp. 46-50.

[8] James, J.S., "What Is FORTH? A Tutorial Introduction," Byte (August, 1980), pp. 100-126.

[9] Katzan, H., Computer Systems Organization and Programming, Science Research Associates, Chicago, 1976.

[10] Katzan, H., Introduction to Computers and Data Processing, D. Van Nostrand Company, New York, 1979.

[11] Katzan, H., Introduction to Computer Science, Petrocelli/Charter, New York, 1975.

[12]   Katzan,   H.,   Introduction   to   Programming
Languages,   Auerbach Publishers, Inc., Philadelphia,
1973.

[13]   Katzan,   H.,   Microprogramming   Primer,
McGraw-Hill Book Company, New York, 1977.

[14] Knuth, D.E., The Art of Computer Programming,
Volume 1, Fundamental Algorithms, Addison-Wesley,
Reading, Massachusetts, 1968.

[15]   Leininger, S.W., "The Radio Shack TRS-80
Microcomputer System," Interface Age (September,
1977), pp. 58-62.

[16] Mandl, M., Fundamentals of Digital Computers,
Prentice-Hall, Inc., Englewood Cliffs, New Jersey,
1958.

[17] Manuel, T., "The hard-disk explosion: high
powered mass storage for your personal computer,"
Byte (August, 1980), pp. 58-70, 138-146.

[18] Miller, A.R., and Miller, J., "Breakforth into
FORTH," Byte (August, 1980), pp. 150-163.

[19] Moore, C.H., "The Evolution of FORTH, an
Unusual Language," Byte (August, 1980), pp. 76-92.

[20] Pollini, S., "Hardware Talk About Hardware,"
Personal Computing (January/February, 1977), pp.
68-70.

[21] von Neumann, J., The Computer and the Brain,
Yale University Press, New Haven, 1958.

[22] Williams, G., "FORTH Glossary," Byte (August,
1980), pp. 186-196.

[23]   Zaks, R., Microprocessors: From Chips to
Systems, SYBEX Incorporated, 1977.

[24] Z80-CPU Technical Manual, Zilog Corporation,
1976.

ANSWERS

Chapter Zero

1. (a) 18
   (b) 17
   (c) 25

2. (a) 21 OK
   (b) 20 OK
   (c) 9 8 3 OK

3. (a) 14 OK
   (b) 13 OK

Chapter One

1. Devices normally treated as "black boxes" in
everyday life are:

   o The fuel injection system in an automobile
   o A modern electronic digital wristwatch
   o An "instant" camera
   o   A   modem   or   multiplexer   for   data
   communications
   o A "laser disk" recording system

In   fact,   most   devices   that   utilize   advanced
technology are commonly used as black boxes.

2. The usual programmable calculator would use a
Harvard   architecture,   since   data   and   program
memories   are   separate   -   i.e., at least as far as
the user is concerned.

3. Read-write memory would be RAM.

4. A computer system in which bandwidth is two
bytes and instruction size is four bytes is a case
where   bandwidth would contribute to less than
optimal performance.   In this example, two fetches

from   storage   would   be   required   to   access   one
instruction.

5. (a) Fetch a word from ROM or RAM. (b) Write a
word to RAM.

Chapter Two

1.   They   both   exist   as   a   finite   list   of
instructions.

2. There are three steps in the greatest common
divisor algorithm.   When applied to the values 35
and 21, nine steps are actually executed.

3. The fields in an assembler language statement
are   the location field, operation code field,
operand field, and the comments field.

4. The output from a language translator includes
the object program and the listing. The output
from an interpreter is a set of computed results.

Chapter Three

1. (a) AB+C-
   (b) AB+C*
   (c) AB*CD/-E+
   (d) AB+CD-/E-
   (e) AY*B+Y*C+
   (f) ABC+*D-E*
   (g) AY*B+Y*C+Y*D+

2.   (a)   (b)

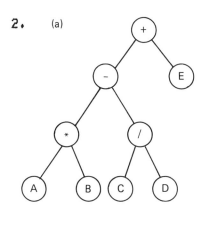
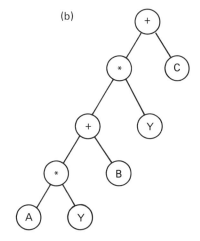

3. (a) 2
   (b) 165
   (c) 22.2

4. Preorder: +A-/BCD
   Postorder: A+B/C-D
   Endorder: ABC/D-+

Chapter Four

1. (a) 2 5 * 3 +
   (b) 2 4 1 + DUP * *
   (c) 5 DUP 1 + DUP 1 + * *
   (d) 4 5 2 */
   (e) 3 4 DUP * SWAP DUP * +

2. (a) 9
   (b) 11

        (c) 27
        (d) -5
        (e) 1
        (f) -3 -4
        (g) 2 1 1
        (h) 9 7 3
        (i) 16 3
        (j) 9 3 7 3
        (k) -1 3 -8 6
        (l) -1 6 -8 3
        (m) 6 -2 -2
        (n) 4 1
        (o) -13
        (p) -6
        (q) 9
        (r) -1 -16
        (s) -63

3. (a) -1
        (b) 5
        (c) 9
        (d) 27
        (e) 16

Chapter Five

1. (a) 1 CONSTANT ONE
        (b) 2 CONSTANT TWO
        (c) 15 CONSTANT DX
        (d) DX TWO * ONE - CONSTANT DY
            or more succinctly
            DX 2 * 1 - CONSTANT DY

2. (a) 321 VARIABLE X
        (b) -6 VARIABLE Y
        (c) X @ Y @ + 173 - VARIABLE W

3. (a) A @ 1 - A !
            or more efficiently
            A DUP @ 1 - SWAP !
            or still more efficiently
            -1 A +!

(b) A @ X @ DUP * * B @ X @ * - C @ + Y !

Chapter Six .

```
1. : 5POWER        ( X)
     DUP DUP       ( X X X)
     *             ( X X**2)
     DUP           ( X X**2 X**2)
     *             ( X X**4)
     *             ( X**5)
   ;
```

2. The page number is assumed to be on the top of the stack.

```
: TITLE
  1 7 VHTAB
  ." INVITATION TO FORTH  Page "
  .
;
```

or alternately

```
: TITLE
  1 1 VHTAB
  6 SPACES
  ." INVITATION TO FORTH  PAGE "
  .
;
```

```
3. : 1+!     ( ADDR )
     1       ( ADDR 1 )
     SWAP    ( 1 ADDR )
     +!
   ;
```


Chapter Seven

```
1. (a) 0  OK
   (b) 0  OK
   (c) 0  OK
```

```
    (d) 1   OK
    (e) 0   OK
    (f) 1   OK
    (g) 0   OK

2. (a) 0   OK
   (b) 0   OK
   (c) 1111111111111111  OK
   (d) 110101111110111  OK
   (e) 1010000000000  OK

3. (a) 10   OK
   (b) 4   OK
   (c) 10
        9
        8
        7
        6   OK

4. Absolute value function

5. (a) : ADD1
          0
          140 57
          DO
            I +
          LOOP
          ;

   (b) : ADD2
          0               ( SUM)
          57              ( INITIAL VALUE)
          BEGIN
            DUP           ( (---|)
            ROT              ( |)
            +               ( | LOOP)
            SWAP            ( |)
            1               ( |)
            +             ( (---|)
            DUP           ( (---|)
            139              ( | CONDITION)
            >             ( (---|)
          UNTIL
```

```
        DROP
      ;

  (c) : ADD3
        0              ( SUM)
        57             ( INITIAL VALUE)
        BEGIN
          DUP          ( (---))
          140            ( 1 CONDITION)
          <            ( (---))
        WHILE
          DUP          ( (---))
          ROT            ( ))
          +              ( ) LOOP)
          SWAP           ( ))
          1              ( ))
          +            ( (---))
        REPEAT
        DROP
      ;
```

Chapter Eight

```
1. : D+!              ( D1 ADDR)
     DUP              ( D1 ADDR ADDR)
     2@               ( D1 ADDR D2)
     5 ROLL 5 ROLL    ( ADDR D2 D1)
     D+               ( ADDR D1+D2)
     ROT              ( D1+D2 ADDR)
     2!
   ;

2. : D1+!      ( ADDR)
     DUP       ( ADDR ADDR)
     2@        ( ADDR D)
     1. D+     ( ADDR D+1)
     ROT       ( D+1 ADDR)
     2!
   ;

3. : D1-!      ( ADDR)
     DUP       ( ADDR ADDR)
```

```
    2@          ( ADDR D)
    1. D-       ( ADDR D-1)
    ROT         ( D-1 ADDR)
    2!
  ;


4. : D1+    ( D)
     1. D+  ( D+1)
  ;


5. : D1-    ( D)
     1. D-  ( D-1)
  ;


6. : D2+    ( D)
     2. D+  ( D+2)
  ;


7. : D2-    ( D)
     2. D-  ( D-2)
  ;
```


Chapter Nine

1. START @ 100 BLANKS

2. HEX 6FC FF3 DECIMAL 1000 CMOVE

3. 2000 11 TYPE

4. 193 2 BASE ! 10111 C! DECIMAL
   Since ASCII is a 7-bit code, the following is
   equivalent:
   65 2 BASE ! 10111 C! DECIMAL

5. 50 BUFFER OK
   VARIABLE BUFLOC OK
   : FILLMAT
     100 0
     DO
       BUFLOC @
       I + DUP
```
```

```
      2 MOD
      IF
        192 SWAP C!
      ELSE
        171 SWAP C!
      THEN
    LOOP
  ; OK

  : PRMAT
    100 0
    DO
      CR
      BUFLOC @
      I + 10 TYPE
    10
    +LOOP
  ;  OK

  : #5
    FILLMAT
    PRMAT
  ;  OK

  #5
  +@+@+@+@+@
  +@+@+@+@+@
  +@+@+@+@+@
  +@+@+@+@+@
  +@+@+@+@+@
  +@+@+@+@+@
  +@+@+@+@+@
  +@+@+@+@+@
  +@+@+@+@+@
  +@+@+@+@+@   OK
```

Or the colon definitions can be combined for
printing as in:

```
  : #5A
    CR
    101 1
    DO
```

```
      I 2 MOD
      IF
        192 EMIT
      ELSE
        171 EMIT
      THEN
      I 10 MOD 0=
      IF
        CR
      THEN
    LOOP
  ; OK
```

#5A
```
@+@+@+@+@+
@+@+@+@+@+
@+@+@+@+@+
@+@+@+@+@+
@+@+@+@+@+
@+@+@+@+@+
@+@+@+@+@+
@+@+@+@+@+
@+@+@+@+@+
@+@+@+@+@+
  OK
```

INDEX

Variable definition, 106-107
VHTAB, 124
VLIST command, 111
von Neumann, J., 40, 210
von Neumann machine, 16

WHILE, 155
Williams, G., 210
Winchester disk, 31
Word, 77-78
Word size, 18

Zaks, R., 210